# WHISTLE BLOWING!

# WHISTLE BLOWING!

## Loyalty and Dissent in the Corporation

Edited with an Introduction and Conclusion by
## ALAN F. WESTIN

With the assistance of
**HENRY I. KURTZ** and **ALBERT ROBBINS**

**McGraw-Hill Book Company**

New York   St. Louis   San Francisco
London   Mexico   New Delhi   Paris   Tokyo   Toronto

Thomas H. Quinn and Michael Hennelly were the
editors of this book. Christine Aulicino was the
designer. Sally Fliess supervised the production. It was
set in Compano by Haddon Craftsman, Inc.
Printed and bound by R. R. Donnelley and Sons, Inc.


**Library of Congress Cataloging in Publication Data**
Main entry under title:

Whistle-blowing.

Sponsored by the Educational Fund for Individual
Rights.
Bibliography: p.
    1. Whistle blowing—United States—Congresses.
I. Westin, Alan F.  II. Kurtz, Henry I.  III. Robbins,
Albert.  IV. Educational Fund for Individual Rights.
HD60.5.U5W47      331'.01      80-15800
ISBN 0-07-069483-4

123456789 RRDRRD 8987654321

# Contents

# Preface

THIS BOOK GROWS OUT of the work of the Educational Fund for Individual Rights, a non-profit foundation organized to conduct research and educational activities about individual rights in corporate employment. The Fund's concentration is on five major issues: rights of employee privacy, fair procedure, freedom of expression, employee participation, and employee access to corporate information. The Fund seeks to analyze new social and individual expectations for greater employee rights in the private workplace; to identify innovative policies being developed by leading managements and to encourage voluntary adoption of such approaches; to examine where legal measures may be needed to ensure general protection of individual rights for corporate employees, and what kinds of legal interventions may be most appropriate in a given context; and to study the actual operations of new voluntary programs or regulatory measures to learn what their effects are on the rights of corporate employees, the effectiveness of corporate management, and the interests of American society as a whole.

As part of the exploration of employee freedom of expression, we organized two panels on "Whistle Blowing, Loyalty, and Dissent in Corporate Life" at the Fund's *First National Seminar on Individual Rights in the Corporation* held in May of 1978. One of these panels, chaired by Harold McGraw, Jr., chairman of the board of McGraw-Hill, featured an analysis by Professor Andrew Hacker of the City University of New York of changing patterns of loyalty by corporate employees over the past 25 years, especially professional and technical employees. The

vii

second panel presented "Experiences of Some Corporate Whistle Blowers." These were personal accounts by Dan Gellert, a pilot for Eastern Air Lines; Barry Castleman, a chemist who worked for Hercules, Inc.; Peter Faulkner, formerly an engineer with Nuclear Services Corporation; and Joseph Rose, a lawyer who worked for Associated Milk Producers, Inc.

The session featuring these whistle blowers drew wide attention from the press, and was rated the most interesting session at the seminar by the 120 corporate executives and 100 representatives from labor unions, government, public-interest groups, foundations, and academia who attended the 1978 seminar. This encouraged us to prepare a special feature that appeared in the September 1978 issue of *The Civil Liberties Review,* of which I was then the editor. This contained expanded versions of the Gellert, Rose, and Faulkner stories as well as other personal accounts dealing with sexual harassment on the job, violations of occupational safety and health requirements, and sex discrimination in promotion policies.

Dozens of telephone calls and letters from other whistle blowers reached us in response to *The Civil Liberties Review* issue. Many public-interest groups wrote us with additional cases in their areas of activity. Simultaneously, whistle blowing in corporations became the subject of several national television programs, business-group forums, and civil liberties conferences in 1978 and 1979.

At that point, we decided to prepare a book that would present both a representative group of current whistle-blowing situations in corporate employment, and a discussion of new organizational and social policies to deal with these issues. This book would not only portray the personal elements in each episode but would also show the major stake that business and American society has in the way corporations respond to charges by their employees that managements are engaging in improper conduct.

Many people helped in the creation of this book, and their assistance is noted with gratitude. Randy Rothenberg, then Staff Editor of *The Civil Liberties Review,* conducted skillful field research into other whistle-blowing cases brought to our attention, and located instances of whistle blowing in other sectors of industry. Alfred Feliu, a student at Columbia Law School and a research assistant at the Fund, was a constant aid in both library and field research, and worked on the Bibliography and Case List in this volume. This book project was coordinated under the calm, efficient direction of the Fund's Executive Director,

Luceil Sullivan. Hope Campbell and Jitka Salaquarda did the manuscript typing. Henry I. Kurtz shared the overall editing of the final chapters with me and wrote the account of Dr. Grace Pierce's case. Henry's professional touch greatly enhanced the clarity and readibility of these narratives.

Albert Robbins, then Managing Editor of *The Civil Liberties Review,* and now Editorial Director at the Educational Fund, brought his intellectual and editorial talents to the development of the initial personal narratives; he also wrote the account of Robert Elliot that appears here and worked on several of the other final chapters.

Our appreciation also goes to Ellen Poler, Director of Developments, Publications Company, McGraw-Hill, who brought the Educational Fund publications to McGraw-Hill, and to Thomas H. Quinn, Editor in Chief for the Social Sciences in McGraw-Hill's Professional and Reference Book Division, who helped greatly in moving this manuscript forward to completion.

Responsibility for the judgments and recommendations contained in the Introduction and Conclusion are solely mine. They do not represent an official position of the Educational Fund for Individual Rights. As an organization, we believe that freedom of expression begins at home, but one of its corollary responsibilities is to make clear which are individual views and which represent official organizational positions.

Since the Fund intends to continue conducting research, issuing reports, and holding seminars on issues of whistle blowing and corporate accountability, we invite readers with experiences in this area to contact us. We would particularly like to hear from corporate employees and executives who have had whistle-blowing experiences, both those successfully resolved within their companies and those that were not. We would also like to hear from corporate managers who can provide us with additional examples of internal mechanisms for dealing responsively with dissent and whistle blowing, and from lawyers who are presently involved in whistle-blowing cases before administrative agencies or in the courts. Because these matters promise to be major business and social-policy issues in the 1980s, we hope to contribute to the public dialogues by bringing such facts and procedures to public attention.

In addition, the Fund will continue to treat whistle-blowing cases and legal developments in our annual national seminars and our clearinghouse publications. Readers interested in learning more about those activities are invited to write to The Educational Fund for Individual Rights, Inc., Suite 826, 475 Riverside Drive, New York, N.Y. 10115.

ALAN F. WESTIN

Professor of Public Law and Government, Columbia University

President, Educational Fund for Individual Rights

# Introduction:
# Why
# Whistle Blowing
# Is on
# the Rise

This book presents the experiences of ten men and women who tried to stop the corporations they worked for from engaging in wrongdoing. In popular parlance, it is a collection of whistle-blowing stories.

Whistle blowers, as we know, are employees who believe their organization is engaged in illegal, dangerous, or unethical conduct. Usually, they try to have such conduct corrected through inside complaint, but if it is not, the employee turns to government authorities or the media and makes the charge public. Usually, whistle blowers get fired. Sometimes, they may be reinstated. Almost always, their experiences are traumatic, and their careers and lives are profoundly affected.

The idea of an employee "blowing a whistle" is actually a rather strange image to use. Normally, someone who blows the whistle is the dominant authority in a social situation. The referee who blows the whistle in a sports contest, for example, is the impartial official who enforces the rules of play. The police officer at an intersection blows a whistle to direct traffic. A lifeguard at the beach blows the whistle to order swimmers in or out of the water. A

1

foreman at a construction site blows a whistle to communicate work orders. In all these situations, the person who has the whistle is the legally invested authority on the spot.

Employees who complain about organizational wrongdoing lack such power. They may be highly paid persons of consummate skill who have worked in their organizations for years, or even decades. But the whistle of authority inside the employing organization belongs to management, and, ultimately, to top management.

Employees who protest corporate wrongdoing are therefore not invoking the whistle of authority but the whistle of desperation. Their action resembles that of a person who blows a whistle to bring help when threatened with assault on the city streets. The hope is that the law will arrive and protect not only the person's rights but the peace and good order of the community. In a society where the law operates well, the hope is also that just wearing the whistle on a street, or threatening to use it in the corporate setting, may serve to ward off misconduct. But, in the real world of urban crime and corporate power, things don't always work that way.

How they work all too often is graphically revealed in the stories of these ten whistle blowers. They represent a wide range of occupations in the corporate work force—auditor, lawyer, nuclear engineer, salesperson, secretary, airline pilot, truck driver, construction worker, research director, and automotive design engineer. The companies they worked for were not small or minor firms but among the nation's largest and best-known corporations, such as Ford Motor Company, Eastern Air Lines, United Parcel Service, Dow Jones, Ortho Pharmaceutical, Nuclear Services Corporation, and Michigan Gas and Electric. And, the wrongdoings these whistle blowers protested were not petty details but issues of major social importance. They dealt with illegal campaign payments to public officials, dangerous nuclear reactors, fraudulent reports to public utility commissions, sex discrimination, unsafe passenger aircraft, potentially harmful drugs, sexual harassment, dangerous construction sites, and unsafe trucks on the highways.

As readers will learn, these employees first tried to voice their concerns within the company's own channels, in the tradition of the organizational loyalist. They met resistance, rejection, and reprisal, and were eventually fired or harassed into resignation or retirement. After their appeals within the company proved fruitless, these people made their protests public, submitting their complaints to various government boards or agencies, or bringing suits for wrongful discharge to the courts to put the truth of what they alleged to the test of independent examination. Though some of the cases are still under adjudication, readers will see that most of the charges these employees made have turned out to be well-founded.

Two years ago, at a panel on loyalty and whistle blowing at the First National Seminar on Individual Rights in the Corporation, the Chairman of McGraw-Hill, Harold McGraw, Jr., declared that "American society needs people ready to blow the whistle on wrongdoing, and corporate top management needs them too." This, he said, raised two key problems: "How can top management keep channels open so that people are encouraged to step forward, and wrongdoing can be corrected from within?" and "How can society invite and protect reporting to public authorities when top corporate people are involved in or fail to correct the wrongdoing?"[1]

In the ideal world of corporate statesmanship described by Mr. McGraw, the employees whose stories are related here, having been vindicated in the public arena, would now be honored members of their corporate staffs. Corporate chief executives would have rebuked management subordinates for unresponsiveness and coverups. The employee's loyalty to the firm in its status as a lawful, ethical organization would have been commended. And, top management attention would have been directed to developing new internal procedures to ensure that such mistakes did not happen again.

Alas, real life in the corporate world does not yet work that way. Only one of these ten individuals is back at his job, and then only because several grievance-system awards forced this management to reinstate the employee. All the others are the walking wounded of conscience; many of them are blacklisted from working in the major corporate community and all are now trying to reshape their careers along new paths.

If these cases represented extraordinary situations—a few rare miscarriages in a basically sound system of corporate administration—we could lament the individual mishaps but remain contented with the system. After all, what are ten cases in a national work force of 80 million employees in the private sector? As long as human beings in executive posts have to make complex decisions about safety, legality, and propriety—in a climate of business competition and sharply rising costs—there are bound to be some "wrong calls," especially when interpersonal factors and work-team relationships are involved.

Unfortunately for American society, the situations illustrated by these stories are far from rare. We selected them to represent the range of experience of almost a hundred such whistle-blowing episodes that we collected, without great difficulty, in planning panels on whistle blowing for two national seminars on employee rights held in 1978 and 1979. Thousands of cases are currently pending before federal regulatory agencies—such as the Equal Employment Opportunity Commission, the Occupational Safety and Health Administration, the Environmental Protection Agency, the Food and Drug Administration, and the Department of Labor. Employees in all these cases are contending that they were fired for bringing violations of employee-protection or public-protection laws to the attention of their own company officials or public authorities. And, where there used to be a few cases brought to the courts each year in which employees asked judges to review firings on the ground that the discharges were in reprisal for refusing to carry out illegal or improper orders, hundreds of such cases are now pending across the country in state and federal courts.

In order to understand why this is happening, and to appreciate the dilemmas that these ten men and women confronted, we need to look briefly at what the law on whistle blowing in private industry was when these employees had to decide whether they would speak out or remain silent. And, we need to sketch in briefly the larger social trends that helped move these employees to choose the hard path of the whistle blower.

From the development of large corporate enterprise in the late 19th century until the middle 1960s, American law and public attitudes supported very broad powers of management in matters of both personnel administration and business policy. In the personnel area, private-sector employees had no right of tenure in their job; they could be fired whenever it was considered necessary by the employer. In addition, a positive duty of loyalty to the firm—its operating rules and procedures, its reputation, and its commercial opportunities—was held by the courts to be an obligation of employment. Standards of personal morality, life-style, dress and grooming, associational activities, and political ideology could be (and were) set by companies as conditions for hiring and advancement. Discrimination in hiring and promotion on the basis of race, religion, sex, age, and handicap was not forbidden in these decades, and it was widely practiced. The law did not protect rights of expression for corporate employees on the job, or even off the job. Procedurally, there was no legal obligation for an employer to provide internal complaint and appeal mechanisms to deal with employee grievances. If employees were dismissed from their jobs and appealed to the courts, the general rule of common law was that no judicial relief was available;

a private employer was free to fire an employee at will, for any reason or even for no reason at all.

The main exception to this hire-and-fire-at-will system in the pre-1960 era involved unionized workers. State and federal legislation beginning in the 1930s protected the rights of individual employees to choose unions to represent them in bargaining with employers over wages, hours, and working conditions. Under this system of "industrial democracy," speech and association that were part of organizing efforts were protected by law. Once employees chose a union, and once working conditions were set by a collective bargaining agreement, formal mechanisms of grievance, appeal, and outside arbitration were provided to handle employee complaints. As for discharge, under the typical union contract an employee can be fired only for "just cause," and the grievance system is available to pass on the validity of management's action. In practice the support actually given to individual employees who claim that their rights of expression or dissent were violated will depend on the willingness of union leaders to press the claim, and judicial interpretation of a union's duty to provide "fair representation." But the 25 million employees in private industry who were covered by collective bargaining agreements in the 1960s clearly enjoyed rights of substance and procedure that were not available to their 55 million nonunionized fellow employees.

This fire-at-will authority of private-sector employers was quite different from the legal situation of *government* employees. Federal and state civil service laws provide for hiring by "merit selection," set "just cause" standards for dismissals, and create systems of hearings and appeals for personnel actions. In addition, the courts have held that government as an employer must follow basic constitutional rules that limit government power in the interests of individual rights. This means that government agencies cannot infringe upon an employee's right to freedom of expression on or off the job unless such conduct disrupts the workplace or interferes with supervisory authority. Under this concept, the right of a state or federal employee to criticize agency policies and actions could be protected by the courts. While there have been important cases where the rights of government whistle blowers were *not* upheld in the courts,[2] and federal legislation on whistle blowing had to be enacted in 1978 to expand the protection of legitimate whistle blowers, the general situation of government employees before the 1970s was at least one in which the law and social mores provided some important protections.

Shifting from personnel management to the area of business policy, the era before the 1970s was a time when American society and the law also supported wide corporate autonomy. It was assumed that most corporate products were safe for consumers; that most substances used in production did not pose serious risks to workers or to the health of people living in nearby communities; that the environment was generally capable of absorbing industrial wastes; and that the manner in which corporations used their funds to influence the political process or secure contracts abroad was not an important issue for public concern. Where occasional problems arose, Americans looked to remedies such as lawsuits for individual damages, limited government regulation, and the "discipline of the market" to provide whatever control was needed over dangerous or improper actions. In this ethos, there was usually little public support or legal protection for an employee who blew the whistle on company practices that were alleged to be harming the public.

During the 1960s and '70s, a series of events and developments took place that shattered these traditional assumptions and drastically altered social attitudes toward the conduct of corporate affairs. The rise of the consumer movement in the '60s focused on dangerous and substandard products, challenging the adequacy of consumer protection under the existing regulatory agency system. The equality movements first attacked racial discrimination and then sex and age discrimination in corporate employment. New findings were made and widely publicized about perils to employee life and health from harmful substances used in the workplace, as well as growing threats of radiation and chemical damage to people living in communities near many types of industrial plants. The environmental protection movement dramatized the harm being done to air, water, and land resources through industrial pollution, and warned of immense dangers ahead if controls over industrial waste disposal were not applied.

In the early 1970s, the Watergate episode demonstrated to an alarmed public the extent to which secret corporate financial contributions were corrupting the American governmental and political process, as well as supporting a system of bribes and corruption in overseas business activities. Throughout this period changes in social values about sex, life-styles, and political beliefs altered the public's sense of the proper line to be drawn between private and public matters; this soon led to the belief that far fewer personal characteristics and behavioral attributes of job applicants and employees should be made the subject of disqualification by employers.

To these developments must be added the new sense of activism and personal moral commitment which grew out of the civil rights, antiwar, consumer, and student protest movements that marked the sixties and seventies. Although this is often portrayed as a mood that affected youth, many middle-aged and older Americans also came to feel a new sense of personal responsibility for confronting unlawful or illegitimate authority with a moral protest. Many people who might not be willing to take such actions themselves came to admire those who did; they recognized such commitment as the vital force that brought about important changes in law and public policy which, in time, won overwhelming public approval. As millions of young people who had been activists or had supported personal activism during their college years moved into corporate employment in the 1970s, a major source of whistle blowing also moved inside the corporate gates.

Along with personal activism came an increased concern among many professional employees in the corporation that they should not be forced to perform services that would clearly violate ethical standards. Such professionals now make up a major segment of the corporate work force—engineers, chemists, computer experts, accountants and auditors, lawyers, physicians, and behavioral scientists. Though their professional codes traditionally spelled out ethical principles to be observed, the issue of whether professionals should refuse to continue working for an employer that directed a violation of professional ethics —the government, a corporation, a university, etc.—became a matter of growing concern among professionals and professional societies in the sixties and seventies.

The public awareness that corporate behavior could have very serious effects on public health, the environment, and the political process, and the new demands for protection of equality and privacy rights in employment led to major legal and organizational changes in the late 1960s and 1970s. First, federal and state laws were enacted to provide new rules for employee protection. Equal employment opportunity laws forbade discrimination in hiring, promotion, or firing on the basis of race, religion, nationality, sex, age, and physical handicap. Rules for occupational safety and health at the workplace were enacted, as well as laws that protected employee pension rights, allowed corporate employees to see the contents of their own personnel records, and forbade employers to interfere with rights of political activity and association by their employees.

Many of these laws contained a provision forbidding an employer to punish an employee for claiming the rights protected in the legislation, or for reporting violations to public authorities. Complaints of employer reprisal could be filed with those government agencies set up to enforce the legislation (such as the Equal Employment Opportunity Commission, Occupational Safety and Health Administration, Department of Labor, etc.). An employer found to have taken reprisals could be ordered to reinstate the employee or to pay damages for improper termination.

Second, a wave of similar federal and state legislation was enacted to protect consumers and the public from improper business practices. These included Truth in Lending Laws, the Fair Credit Reporting Act and Equal Credit Opportunity Act, the Environmental Protection Act, the Fair Campaign Practices Acts (on corporate political contributions), and the Foreign Corrupt Practices Act (on illegal overseas payments). In addition, there were amendments and new laws dealing with protection of the public in particular industries, such as registration of new drugs by the pharmaceutical industry or regulation of operations by the nuclear power industry. Many of these public protection laws also contained antireprisal provisions that forbade the firing of an employee for reporting violations to public authorities. The antireprisal rights were not well-known at first, and it took time for employees to learn how to use them. But by the end of the seventies, they began to change supervisory relationships in some important ways, as several of the stories in this book will show.

In another major legal development, some state and federal courts in the 1970s began to carve out an important exception to the common-law doctrine supporting management's power to fire-at-will. The courts had traditionally upheld management's absolute right to dismiss because of several judgments: the private employer's right to organize and administer the work force as it saw best to achieve efficiency; the concept that no one has a right of tenure in private employment unless there is an express contract; and the difficulties that judges would have in passing on disputed personnel decisions. Some judges also warned that accepting such cases would "choke the courts" with personnel litigation.[3]

Beginning in the mid-1970s, a few courts began to hold that where important "public policy considerations" would be offended by refusing to question the employer's action, the courts could intervene. Courts in Oregon and Pennsylvania, for example, held that damages could be awarded where employees were fired for performing jury service;[4] to hold otherwise, the courts said, would defeat the public policy of encouraging individuals to do their civic duty. Similarly, a New Hampshire court granted damages to a woman who had been fired when she refused to go out on a date with her foreman.[5] The court said that upholding such a "bad faith" or "malicious" discharge would not be in the best interest of the economic system or the public good, even in the absence of a statutory prohibition against sexual harassment. A West Virginia court rejected the fire-at-will doctrine when a bank dismissed an officer who revealed to authorities that the bank was intentionally overcharging customers in violation of federal and state consumer protection laws.[6] The court said that where the state legislature had declared a public policy in favor of protecting consumers, it would undermine that policy to let a regulated bank dismiss one of its employees who attempted to see that the law was obeyed.

Parallel decisions also began to appear in the federal courts. A federal appeals court held that an employee fired for publishing an article criticizing his corporate employer (and also the union) could not be legally discharged where the employer was a defense contractor for the federal government.[7] The court found that the article was not defamatory and it did not advocate wildcat strikes; therefore, the employee's right of free speech had to prevail over the company's concern that such expressions might cause a strike. In effect, the presence of a defense contract led the court to apply the "balancing" standard used in free speech cases involving government employment.

In a group of cases decided in the late 1970s, several courts said that _if_ the employee could prove that a dismissal had been prompted by motives or reasons that would contravene "public policy," there would be grounds for judicial intervention. These decisions included the cases of an employee who charged that her firing was because of a protest against racial discrimination,[8] an X-ray technician who said she was fired for refusing to perform a procedure that was legally supposed to be done only by a licensed physician or nurse,[9] and a research director of a pharmaceutical firm who alleged that she was driven out of her job because she would not approve a dangerous drug-testing and marketing plan.[10]

While this recent group of judicial decisions represents a very important development, it is still a minority trend. Most courts during the 1970s still applied the traditional fire-at-will rule. For example, one court refused to look into the claim that several auditors had been discharged for refusing to approve bills for services that were being performed by a contractor as kickbacks for several top executives.[11] Judges refused to intervene when a steel company sales executive was discharged for complaining to management about a faulty steel product.[12] They left untouched a case in which an auto engineer alleged he was fired for refusing management directions to give false information to the government.[13] And, a court declined to review the firing of an employee of a hospital for allegedly refusing an order to alter medical reports.[14] In short, though there were some states willing to reconsider the employment-at-will doctrine, most courts were not yet willing to do this as a matter of judicial initiative.

A final trend has been the development of considerable ferment in the corporate world in the late 1970s in response to new demands for employee rights outside the unionized sector. Several dozen companies with reputations for anticipative management have voluntarily instituted new policies that recognize rights of employee privacy and adopt new procedures for hearing employee complaints. Some of these also provide codes of voluntary self-disclosure to make more information about corporate actions and policies available to employees and the general public, and have developed high-participation techniques of making decisions or organizing work. By the end of the 1970s, however, only a small fraction of the 10,000 largest corporations in the nation had developed such innovative policies. The great majority of firms, except where required by employee protection laws, were still operating with personnel policies that embodied the management-discretion philosophy of the pre-1970 era, and these were administered in that spirit by thousands of managers.

As a result, the 1970s were marked by the large number of cases in which the public has learned that employees decided *not* to speak out publicly against unsafe products, dangerous procedures, illegal payoffs, sexual harassment, and other illegalities. The tragic way we know about these cases is that after serious harm was inflicted on customers, passengers, workers, local residents, or the general public, government agencies or court actions revealed that some employees had warned that these things would happen. When they were ignored or overruled by management, these employees decided to swallow the whistle. It is worth noting three examples of such conduct during the 1970s.

In 1973, Thomas A. Robertson, the director of development of Firestone Tire, sent top management a memo warning that "We are making an inferior quality radial tire which will subject us to belt-edge separation at high mileage."[15] Ignoring this and other memos from Firestone's technical staff, the management kept producing the 500, selling over 24 million of the tires in the next five years. Despite incidents of blowouts and separations that other tires did not suffer, and despite reports about poor performance to Firestone by major customers such as General Motors and Atlas Tire Company, the Firestone management kept issuing statements that the 500s were completely safe. By 1979, as *Time* magazine recently reported, blowouts of the tires had caused "at least 41 deaths" and hundreds of serious injuries. The company has already had to replace about 3 million of the tires and many more replacements will have to be made. The Securities and Exchange Commission is currently conducting an investigation to determine whether the failure of Firestone's top executives and technical experts to disclose the 500s defects earlier constitutes a violation of federal law. In addition, Firestone's liability insurance could be at least partially invalidated if it is shown that company officials knew of the defects and continued producing the tires. In a lawsuit last year, involving two deaths and a survivor who is now a paraplegic, Firestone made a $1.4 million settlement out of court. Over 250 such personal liability suits are currently pending and it is estimated that judgments of well over $100 million may eventually be recovered. If Mr. Robertson and other executives or technicians who knew of the serious flaws in the 500s had blown the whistle, major costs in life and property could have been averted and Firestone's reputation would not have been disgraced. (A recent comedy routine on television had one man ask his friend, "Did you get your brother-in-law anything for Christmas?" "Oh, yes," came the reply, "I got the bastard a Ford Pinto with Firestone 500 radials. . . .")

In a major scandal now developing in the asbestos industry, internal company documents recently obtained by a congressional committee show that the industry had far more knowledge of the harmful effects of asbestos from the 1930s onward than they have admitted, and well before the time—the mid 1960s—when the companies said they first learned of serious health hazards.[16] A recent United Press International report on the internal documents says they "show that one asbestos company did not tell its workers when physical examinations found they had asbestosis, a disease fatal unless treated early; that another manufacturer discharged a medical consultant and ignored his warnings about asbestos exposure, and that the industry suppressed findings in the 1930s and 1940s that asbestos exposure could be dangerous to humans." As a result of deaths and disabling diseases contracted not only by workers making asbestos but also workers using asbestos in general construction and persons exposed to asbestos flaking in schools and other buildings, more than 1,000 lawsuits have already been filed against the asbestos companies, totaling more than $2 billion in claims. Yet none of the company medical directors and physicians who found asbestosis in employee physical examinations blew the whistle publicly on company concealment of the findings from the employees or the suppression of medical trend data from the public.

Or, take the case of Hooker Chemical Company. Engineers, chemists, plant managers, and senior executives of Hooker, a subsidiary of Occidental Petroleum Corporation, knew in 1975 and 1976 that the Hooker plant in Lathrop, California, was polluting underground water supplies with toxic pesticides. They also knew that its plant in White Springs, Florida, was seriously violating air pollution limits in its smokestack emissions.[17] But the company, caught up in a cost-cutting campaign, refused to cure the problems. Commenting on company documents obtained during a civil suit and various federal investigations, a New York *Times* analysis noted that "Hooker's own environmental engineers were pleading for $2.58 million to stem the dumping [in California]. . . ."

One report in the spring of 1965 by the Lathrop plant's chief environmental engineer, Robert Edson, told management: "Recently published California State Water Quality Control Laws clearly state that we cannot percolate chemicals to ground water. The laws are extremely stringent about pesticides. We percolate all of our gypsum water, our pesticide wastes and 1 percent to 3 percent of our product to the ground in the form of production losses. Not only must we stop this by law, but it will recover $20,000 to $40,000 a month in losses." His memo went on to be more specific. "Our neighbors are concerned about the quality of water from their wells. Recently water from our waste pond percolated into our neighbor's field. His dog got in it, licked himself, and died. Our laboratory records indicate that we are slowly contaminating all wells in our area and two of our own wells are contaminated to the point of being toxic to animals and humans. THIS IS A TIME BOMB THAT WE MUST DE-FUSE." But Mr. Edson and his fellow environmental engineers at Hooker Chemical did not report these violations to state or federal authorities, or to the news media. Only when pollution by Hooker reached major proportions and its harm to the Love Canal area of Niagara Falls, New York, became a national cause célèbre did the truth finally begin to emerge.

Lamenting the high incidence of such non-whistle blowing by corporate personnel, and the harm done to the public by their silence, Ralph Nader has commented:

> Corporate employees are among the first to know about industrial dumping of mercury or fluoride sludge into waterways, defectively de-

signed automobiles, or undisclosed adverse effects of prescription drugs and pesticides. They are the first to grasp the technical capabilities to prevent existing product or pollution hazards. But they are very often the last to speak out, much less to refuse to be recruited for acts of corporate or governmental negligence or predation.[18]

Nader voiced that judgment in January of 1971, at a conference that reported on whistle blowing in both government and industry. In the corporate area, the conference report featured the stories of more than a dozen corporate employees and executives who had blown the whistle between 1965 and 1971 on "corrupt, illegal, fraudulent, or harmful activity" by their corporate employers.[19] The list included a safety inspector for General Motors; a construction engineer for Brown and Root; a sales executive for U.S. Steel; a scientific writer for B. F. Goodrich; a medical director at Squibb Pharmaceuticals; an assistant division manager at Lockheed Aircraft; a welding supervisor for Stone and Webster Engineering; a pump operator at Jones & Laughlin Steel Company; a project engineer for Proctor and Gamble; and seven manufacturing employees of Colt Industries.

These cases of the 1960s represent what might be called the first stage of the contemporary whistle-blowing phenomenon in American industry. It was led primarily by employees who were impelled to action during the consumer-protection, civil rights, and antiwar movements of the 1960s. They were the first people to break out of the "Organization Man" ethos of total company loyalty that corporate policy dictated and social mores accepted in the forties and fifties. Almost all of these first-stage protesters lost their jobs, and also any protests they took to the courts. The judicial doctrines upholding employment-at-will and the very limited number of antireprisal provisions in federal and state legislation at that time made legal recourse almost impossible. But these first-stage whistle blowers had made an important contribution, especially in helping to focus public attention on the need to enact more detailed laws to deal with pollution, maintenance of dangerous workplaces, marketing of unsafe products, and continuation of discriminatory personnel practices.

The second stage of corporate whistle blowing, from the early 1970s down to the present, has been marked by two parallel trends: the enactment of dozens of major new employee-protection and public-protection laws by Congress and the states, and a steady rise in whistle-blowing episodes. The fact that whistle blowing increased while the laws defining and forbidding corporate misconduct also increased may seem paradoxical. But the explanation lies in the fact that many corporate managements were still operating under the old assumptions and that effective legal-appeal mechanisms outside the corporate walls had not yet taken hold. The result was that most whistle blowers of 1970–1979 fared only a little better than their predecessors.

This sketch of legal doctrines and organizational approaches prior to 1970 and the changes that began to unfold during the 1970s provides the essential backdrop for our cases. Now, it is time to read the stories of ten corporate employees who embodied the new forces we have described, and to see what happened to them when they decided they had to speak up.

## NOTES

1. *Proceedings of the National Seminars on Individual Rights in the Corporation, 1978, 1979, 1980* (to be published).

2. For accounts of government employees fired or disciplined for their efforts to expose illegal or improper conduct, see Ralph Nader, Peter Petkas, and Kate Blackwell (editors), *Whistle Blowing* (New York: Grossman, 1972), and David W. Ewing, *Freedom Inside the Organization* (New York: Dutton, 1977).

3. For a sample of the employment-at-will decisions over the past decade, see *Geary v. U.S. Steel Corporation*, 319 A. 2d 174 (1974); *Percival v. General Motors Corporation*, 539 F. 2d 1126 (8th Cir. 1976); *Trombetta v. Detroit*, Toledo and Ironton R. Co., 265 N.W. 2d 385 (1978).

4. *Nees v. Hocks*, 536 P. 2d 512 (1975), Oregon; *Reuther v. Fowler & Williams, Inc.,* 386 A. 2d 119 (1978), Pennsylvania.

5. *Monge v. Beebe Rubber Company*, 316 A. 2d 549 (1974).

6. *Harless v. First National Bank in Fairmont*, 246 S.E. 2d 270 (1978).

7. *Holodnak v. Avco–Lycoming Division*, 514 F. 2d 285 (2d Cir. 1975).

8. *Davis v. U.S. Steel Supply*, 581 F. 2d 335 (3d Cir. 1978).

9. *O'Sullivan v. Mallon*, 390 A. 2d 149 (1978).

10. *Pierce v. Ortho Pharmaceuticals*, 166 N.J. Super. 335, 399 A. 2d 1023 (1979).

11. *Perdue v. J.C. Penney*, 470 F. Supp. 1234 (1979).

12. *Geary*, note 3 *supra.*

13. *Percival*, note 3 *supra.*

14. *Hinricks v. Tranquillaire Hospital,* 352 S.E. 2d 1138 (1977).

15. "Forewarnings of Fatal Flaws: But Firestone Continued to Sell a Troubled Tire," *Time,* June 25, 1979, 58–61.

16. "Papers Reportedly Show Effort to Hide Asbestos Risk," New York *Times,* November 13, 1978; Morton Mintz, "Workers Unwarned of Asbestos Peril, Lawmakers Learn," *Washington Post,* November 16, 1979, p. B11.

17. Donald G. McNeil, Jr., "Hooker Corp. Papers Indicate Management Sanctioned Polluting," New York *Times,* August 5, 1979, p. 1; "Dumped Hooker Pesticides Poisoned Wells on Coast," *ibid.,* August 6, 1979, p. A15; Reply by company, "Hooker Was Not 'Careless,' " Letters, *ibid.,* August 18, 1979; Irvin Molotsky, "State Accuses Hooker Corp. of Illegal Dumping on L.I.," *ibid.,* September 1, 1979, p. 21.

18. Ralph Nader, Peter J. Petkas, and Kate Blackwell (editors), *Whistle Blowing* (New York: Grossman, 1972), p. 4.

19. *Ibid.*

# Insisting on Safety in the Skies

## Dan Gellert

I had been a pilot for 25 years, the last ten of them
with Eastern Air Lines, when, in 1972, I blew the
whistle on a serious defect in the new Lockheed
1011 wide-body aircraft. At the time, in addition to
flying regularly scheduled flights for Eastern, I was
also involved in flight training and engineering
safety.

You might say that Eastern created their own
monster in me because the company sent me to the
Air Force Safety School, the Army Crash Survival
Investigators Course, and Aerospace Systems Safety,
a highly regarded training course given at the
University of Southern California. Because of my
safety training, I was able to spot a serious design
problem in the L-1011, which was first being
introduced into commercial service at that time.
When I tried to alert top management at Eastern
about the defect, my warnings were ignored, and a
few months later, the problem played a key role in
the crash of an Eastern L-1011 in which 103 people
died.

Today, seven years later, after three lawsuits
and a $1.6 million judgment against Eastern in my

favor, I am still with Eastern. I have no regrets about what I have done, but I have learned that those who blow the whistle often pay a price. In my case, that price was a five-year campaign of harassment waged against me by Eastern that disrupted my private life and nearly cost me my professional reputation.

It all started in the summer of 1972 when I was going through flight-training school for the L-1011. My roommate was in a simulator when the autopilot and flight instrumentation disengaged, crashing the flight simulator on a practice landing approach. Even though simulated crashes don't cause injuries, my roommate assumed that the mock crash was due to some design problem in the L-1011 autopilot system, and he reported the incident to Eastern's flight-operations people. His report was ignored.

The problem with the L-1011 autopilot system was much more insidious than a potential engine fire or the possibility of a wing or an engine falling off—like the defect in the engine mounts that caused the crash of an American Air Lines DC-10 at Chicago's O'Hare Airport in the summer of 1979. Defects such as these are generally acknowledged to be safety hazards. The L-1011 defect, however, involved the complex interaction between the crew and the autopilot and related instrumentation which they relied upon to conduct a safe approach to a runway when landing the aircraft.

I became acutely aware of the problem in the L-1011 autopilot system in September 1972. I was flying an L-1011 with 230 passengers aboard, cruising on autopilot at 10,000 feet, when I accidentally dropped my flight plan. As I bent down to pick it up, my elbow bumped the control stick in front of me. Suddenly, the plane went into a steep dive —something that shouldn't have occurred. Fortunately, I was able to grab the control stick and ease the plane back onto course.

What had happened, I realized, was that in bumping the stick, I had tripped off the autopilot. Instead of holding the plane at 10,000 feet, it had switched from its "command mode" to "control wheel steering." As a result, when the stick moved forward, causing the plane to dive, the autopilot, rather than holding the aircraft on course, held it in the dive.

There was no alarm system to warn me that the plane was off course. If I hadn't retrieved my flight plan quickly, observing the dive visually when I sat up in my seat, the plane could easily have crashed. Even more alarming, as I eased the plane back onto course, I noticed that the autopilot's altimeter indicated that the plane was flying at 10,000 feet—the instrumentation was giving me a dangerously false reading.

I made a verbal report on the near disaster to an Eastern management official who told me, "We'll look into it." I told him, "You'd better before we kill a bunch of people." And that's exactly what happened barely three months later.

On December 29, 1972, an Eastern Air Lines L-1011 crashed, killing 103 people. The plane was making its landing approach at Miami International Airport when a light bulb that is supposed to come on when the landing gear is down and locked into place failed to light up. The crew switched the plane, then at 2,000 feet, to autopilot and went to investigate whether the landing gear had come down or not. Four minutes later, the aircraft crashed into the Everglades.

When I learned of the accident, I was certain that the defect in the autopilot system must have contributed to the accident. The control stick could easily have been disengaged, and the crew, distracted by the landing-gear problem, might have failed to notice the plane's descent. Even if the crew had been monitoring their instrumentation, they would have received a false reading, at least from the autopilot altimeter. And, if the weather was bad that night—the ground obstructed by clouds or fog—there would have been little or no time for the crew to observe their descent visually and react accordingly.

I outlined these problems with the L-1011 autopilot in a two-page written evaluation I sent to the top three people at Eastern Air Lines— Frank Borman, then vice president of operations; Floyd Hall, chairman of the board; and Samuel Higgenbottom, president of operations. I sent my memo out almost immediately after the Florida crash. It wasn't until February that I received a reply—Frank Borman wrote me that it was "pure folly" to say that one procedure could cause an accident. I realized that I had to do something else.

I sent copies of my two-page evaluation to my union, the Airline Pilots Association (ALPA), and to the National Transportation Safety Board (NTSB), which was about to conduct a hearing into the cause of the crash. My main concern was not the crash itself, but the horrors that potentially lay in store for Eastern if it failed to correct the defect: more crashes, numerous deaths, destruction of property, and astronomical punitive damages levied against the company for failing to correct the problem.

The NTSB called me to discuss the crash shortly after they received my letter. They agreed with me that the autopilot was a cause of concern in their investigation, and they sent me a subpoena to testify at their hearing. Many of my friends at Eastern urged me to ignore the subpoena and not appear. Instead, I ignored these so-called friends.

At the NTSB hearing, I stressed the problem with the L-1011 autopilot. Most other witnesses, however, blamed the crash on pilot error; after all, these witnesses maintained, it's the pilot's responsibility to monitor flight instruments. In June 1973, the NTSB released its "probable cause" report on the crash. The report stated: "The probable cause of this accident was the failure of the flight crew to monitor the flight instruments during the final minutes of the flight, and to detect an unexpected defect soon enough." In other words, the NTSB found that a defect in the autopilot caused the crash, but still attributed the tragedy to "pilot error" because the crew did not act to correct the defect in the few seconds available to them.

The NTSB decision, of course, was just what Eastern and Lockheed were hoping for—instead of having to pay punitive damages to the survivors of the crash victims, the manufacturer and the airline only had to pay compensatory damages. I was later to learn that there had been collusion between Eastern and the NTSB to cover up the real cause of the crash and to conceal the fact that Eastern had been warned about the defect in the autopilot in time to have prevented the disaster.

The day after the Everglades crash, Eastern's head of 1011 flight training, Thad Royall (who was promoted to a management position even after he had been involved in a fiery crash of two airplanes on a runway while serving as a pilot), together with an NTSB investigator, went into the flight simulator and flew the same flight pattern as the crashed aircraft. The simulator crashed at almost the same spot as the real plane. Royall and the investigator decided to keep the incident quiet. Three months later, at a meeting attended by Borman, Royall, and other Eastern executives, Borman announced his decision not to modify the design of the L-1011 autopilot because "the FAA had approved it." It wasn't until July, after the NTSB released its findings, that Eastern quietly decided to modify the autopilot design.

In retrospect, I believe that considerable pressure was placed on the NTSB by the Nixon White House to find for "pilot error" in the Florida crash. The Nixon administration had just secured for Lockheed, which had been on the verge of bankruptcy, a huge government-guaranteed loan. Lockheed's long-term ability to repay the loan depended, to a large degree, on the company's success in selling its L-1011. The head of the FAA at the time was Alexander Butterfield, the former Nixon White House aide who revealed the existence of Nixon's taping system to the Senate Select Committee on Watergate. From people I've spoken with, I've had some very strong indications that the White House gave some very explicit instructions to the NTSB on how to handle the investigations so as not to cast Lockheed in an unfavorable light.

The result was that the crew was blamed for a situation in which the blame should have at least been shared by the manufacturer. There is one other curious aspect to Lockheed's responsibility in the Florida crash. Months later, in the suit for damages stemming from the tragedy, Lockheed made compensatory-damage payments to the families of the victims, including the flight crew—something they certainly wouldn't have done if the sole cause of the crash was the flight crew's negligence.

I didn't know any of this when the NTSB handed down its findings, and at the time I tried just to forget the entire incident. But in December 1973, I was flying on an L-1011 when the autopilot disengaged twice when it shouldn't have. The second time it happened, we were coming in for a landing in Atlanta. The plane broke out of the dense clouds covering the city that day at 200 feet. The command bars showed the pilot that he was on the proper glide slope at the correct altitude—500 feet. Below us was a densely populated neighborhood. The crew had to engage full take-off power in order to make the runway and land safely. If the cloud cover had been any lower, the plane would have crashed.

I felt I had to take some further action. Over a year had passed since I made my initial complaint about the autopilot system to Eastern, and it still hadn't been modified. One plane had already crashed because of the defect, and if my experience over Atlanta was any indication, more crashes were likely to follow. (Unknown to me at the time, Eastern was in the process of modifying its L-1011s. The amount of pressure necessary to disengage the autopilot was increased, and the warning light in the cockpit was altered so that it would alert the pilot should the autopilot disengage on an instrument-landing approach.)

I wrote a 12-page petition to the NTSB explaining the continuing problem with the L-1011 autopilot, and I requested the board to modify its findings in the Florida crash. I sent a copy of this petition to Frank Borman as well. I still considered myself to be a loyal Eastern employee, and I thought it was possible that Borman just wasn't fully informed of the problem. I realized that I might be making trouble for myself, but I didn't see any other way to deal with the situation in good conscience. After all, lives were at stake: my own, those of other Eastern employees, and, most important, Eastern's passengers.

The next thing I knew Eastern demoted me to co-pilot. Twice a year pilots bid on a base, a position, or a particular aircraft. Eastern, in a letter sent to my home addressed "Dear Occupant," said that I had returned a blank bid sheet. As a result, Eastern said, they had no choice but to give me a co-pilot slot. Since I had not returned a blank bid sheet at all,

I realized that I was being penalized by the company for my petition to the NTSB. I sent a letter of protest to Frank Borman.

In the meantime, the NTSB responded to my petition by querying Eastern about what it was doing to modify the L-1011. Eastern informed the board that it was making the necessary alterations in the aircraft—which was true—and the board dropped the matter. In a letter of January 24, 1974, to Frank Borman, who by this time had become Eastern's president, W.R. Krepling, then the company's vice president for flight operations, outlined to Borman what was being done to make the L-1011 safer. He also discussed my petition. "Much of what Gellert says is true," Krepling wrote, and he recommended that Borman not respond to my letter.

My confrontation with Eastern management placed me under a great deal of stress. I decided that perhaps I should leave Eastern for a while, if not for good (I was permitted to take a three-year leave of absence from my job under ALPA's contract with Eastern). At the time, the FBI was recruiting agents who had a knowledge of Eastern Europe. Since I had been raised in Hungary, I decided to apply. Several months went by. I had passed my FBI interview and was all set to join the bureau when I received Frank Borman's long-awaited reply to my letter of protest—he personally grounded me for medical reasons.

The letter was astonishing. Eastern questioned my ability to fly an aircraft since, they said, I had written so many letters concerning flight safety. Obviously, they maintained, there was something wrong with me mentally. In my quarter of a century as a pilot, I had never had a complaint from either a passenger or a crew member about my flying. My safety record was impeccable—I had never so much as blown a tire. And there was certainly nothing wrong with my mental faculties. I was furious.

It seemed to me that Eastern's decision to ground me was closely connected with my request for a leave of absence. Rather than leave Eastern and join the FBI—which might have conveyed the impression that Borman had some justification for grounding me—I decided to remain with Eastern to salvage my reputation. The only way to protect myself, I felt, was to file a grievance against the company.

Under ALPA's contract with Eastern Air Lines, any pilot grievance that involves the terms of the contract must be brought before the Eastern Airlines Pilots System Board of Adjustment—a body established by the contract which has the power to settle any dispute. When a complaint is lodged, the System Board initially convenes as a four-man body: two members come from ALPA and two members come from Eastern management. Should the four-man board become dead-locked, an independent arbiter is added to settle the matter.

My grievance against Eastern took seven months to decide. Ulti-mately, the System Board found that Eastern had no basis on which to ground me, and early in 1975, I was reinstated as a pilot and I resumed my duties with Eastern. ALPA's assistance was invaluable to me throughout the grievance process, especially the talents of their attor-ney, John Loomis, who represented me before the board.

Once I was reinstated, however, it became obvious that I needed additional legal help. Shortly after I resumed flying for Eastern, the company sent me a series of letters threatening to fire me if I ever complained about safety to an outside agency again. I didn't like the idea of Eastern's threats; they were contrary to the ALPA contract and to federal air regulations. I consulted with an attorney who advised me that the best way to forestall Eastern would be to sue them. With his help, I filed a $1.5 million civil suit against the airlines for "intentional infliction of mental stress."

Civil suits normally take months and months to wind their way through the court process. Eastern management may have been unaware that I had even filed the action, that is, until my attorney took deposi-tions from Frank Borman and other senior management at Eastern in June 1976. Within two weeks, Eastern began a series of "discipline" actions against me that were to make my life miserable.

In mid-July, Eastern's chief pilot in Miami, who is in charge of scheduling flight crews, informed me that he was suspending me for two days. He told me that I had been unavailable for a flight three weeks earlier that I should have flown. I filed a grievance on this charge, and the System Board ultimately found in my favor at the four-man level. The board said that Eastern's policy had always been to suspend a pilot at the time an incident took place, not three weeks later. They dismissed the suspension and ordered Eastern to reimburse me for two days' pay.

The hearing on the two-day suspension took place in Miami, 300 miles south of my home in Cocoa Beach, in November 1976. Since I had to attend the hearing, I couldn't fly my normal flights. I called Eastern's crew-scheduling office and asked for time off. Instead, I was handed a two-week suspension for being unavailable to pilot a trip—the same spurious charge that forced me to be in Miami in the first place. I filed yet another grievance, and again the System Board found in my favor.

Eastern was still determined to discipline me, however. In January 1977, I completed a flight at 11:30 at night and checked in with crew scheduling, Eastern's standard procedure. The scheduling office told me that I was slated to pilot another flight four hours later. I told the man on duty that I thought it would be unsafe for me to pilot an aircraft with, at best, three hours' sleep. I told him that I would be back at the airport in time to fly the trip, but that I didn't want to take the assignment unless he was unable to get someone to replace me. When I returned to the crew-scheduling office four hours later, I was told that I had been removed from the flight. Two days after that, the chief pilot suspended me for a month.

I filed still another grievance against Eastern, and once again the System Board found in my favor. In its decision, the System Board was highly critical of the company. A previous board decision had established that pilots were entitled to a minimum of eight hours' rest between flights. So Eastern should never have scheduled me in the first place. Aside from that, federal air regulations required that a pilot should remove himself from a flight if, for any reason—fatigue, illness, or whatever—he feels that he is unable to fly an aircraft. Eastern's long-standing policy in such decisions, the board found, was to rely on "pilot self-assessment."

Instead of relying on my judgment of my own ability to fly, Eastern was forcing me to fly its aircraft in what I considered an unsafe manner—endangering its passengers—all in an effort to discredit me before my civil suit came to trial. When I resumed my flight duties following my one-month suspension (it took nearly a year for the System Board to actually decide my grievance), I was again scheduled to fly with inadequate rest on numerous occasions. At this point, with a jury trial of my suit scheduled for September, I didn't want to argue with the chief pilot about it. Why give him an opportunity to suspend me for an even longer period of time? I flew the trips.

On May 27, 1977, three months prior to the court hearing, I piloted a flight into Kennedy Airport in New York. As I was getting into the limousine that was taking the flight crew to our hotel, my name was announced over the airport's PA system, requesting me to report to the chief pilot's office. When I got there, I was told to return immediately to Florida. Although I was in uniform, the chief pilot told me that I was to fly back home in the passenger section and under no circumstances enter the cockpit of the plane.

When I got back to Florida, Eastern informed me that they were grounding me indefinitely. The company said that I was to be re-evaluated, and that I would be notified when to report to Eastern's doctors for a thorough medical examination. On June 27 I received a registered letter from Eastern ordering me to report to their doctors in

Miami at 9:00 A.M. on the morning of June 27. If I didn't report for the examination, the letter stated, I would be grounded without pay (until June 27, even though I had been grounded for a month, I was receiving sick leave).

The letter was delivered to me in Cocoa Beach at 11:00 A.M., two hours after I was scheduled to appear in Miami. There was no way I could possibly have complied with Eastern's demand—I simply didn't know about it until it was too late. Nevertheless, Eastern went ahead and revoked my sick-leave pay—they called it a disciplinary action for failing to appear for my medical examination—and for the next year, I had no source of income.

The motives behind Eastern's summary grounding of me became very apparent when my civil suit was tried in September 1977. Eastern's entire defense rested on the testimony of one of my doctors and the neutral doctor who had examined me when I was first grounded in 1974. (Under the ALPA contract, a pilot has the right to be examined by his own doctor in addition to an Eastern doctor. If the two disagree on a diagnosis, a neutral doctor is asked to examine the pilot in order to resolve the dispute.) Both of these doctors appeared on Eastern's behalf, and Eastern's entire defense was that these doctors had recommended a medical reevaluation of me based on new evidence put before them. Not once did Eastern challenge the truth of the charges I had made to the NTSB.

My lawyer took Eastern's defense and turned it around on them. He demonstrated to the jury that my medical grounding had nothing to do with any alleged mental problem; in fact, he showed that I had never even been examined by a physician prior to my grounding. Instead, my lawyer said, Eastern's grounding of me was another in a long series of actions aimed at discrediting me in the eyes of the jury. My real problem, said my lawyer, was that I had tried to have a serious safety problem in the L-1011 aircraft corrected.

I won my case, and Eastern was stunned at the jury's decision. In addition to the $1.5 million in damages ($1.25 million in punitive damages) I was seeking, the jury awarded me an extra $100,000 to penalize Eastern for its transparent attempt at discrediting me. The trial judge called Eastern's actions against me "outrageous and mischievous."

While I couldn't have been more pleased with the outcome of the law suit, it was really a pyrrhic victory. Eastern appealed the judgment, and a Florida circuit court set aside the $1.6 million verdict on a technical issue of tort law. Today, two-and-a-half years later, the case is still tied up in appellate courts and I have received no money from it. In the meantime, I was still grounded—without pay—and unable to earn a living. Eastern's claims about my mental incapacity effectively kept me from working for any other airline. Eastern told me that they wouldn't even answer letters of reference sent to them by prospective employers about me. Eastern did make one offer, though. They asked me to sign a letter relieving them of any liability in the civil suit; in return, they said they would reinstate me as a pilot. In other words, in exchange for my job, I was to relinquish any claim against the company, including the $1.5 million the jury awarded me. I told Eastern no thanks.

As soon as I had been grounded without pay the previous June, I had filed yet another grievance with the System Board seeking reinstatement. The System Board asked that I be examined by Eastern's doctors, and I went to the Eastern medical department twice: in October 1977 and in April 1978. In both instances, I passed the examinations. Eastern refused to reinstate me, however. Instead, they sent me to an outside consultant in Chicago who did a lot of work for the FAA. Eastern sent this doctor 500 pages of transcripts from the civil suit that they claimed demonstrated my mental problems. When I got to Chicago, the doctor showed me the transcripts—they had been carefully edited to exclude any claims counter to Eastern's argument. The doctor examined me thoroughly, and after three months of reading through the mountains of court documents, rendered a 25-page report that pronounced me fit to fly.

In the meantime, my grievance came before a four-man System Board. Eastern admitted before this board that there was no way I could have complied with their request for me to appear in Miami for a medical examination. Even so, the company claimed that my grounding was a disciplinary action, and they refused to reinstate me or to pay me sick leave.

The grievance went before a five-man board a few months later, and for the fifth time in as many grievances, the board found in my favor. The neutral arbiter in the case found that Eastern had disregarded long-standing policy in grounding me for medical reasons without a prior examination. The arbiter went on to say that once a man has been grounded for medical reasons, he is on sick leave and cannot be disciplined. Eastern's so-called discipline in my case, the arbiter said, was completely unwarranted since post office records showed that Eastern's notice of my medical examination was delivered after it was to have taken place.

At several points in the proceeding, Eastern went one step further. Eastern's attorney characterized my year-long grounding as "personal leave"—in fact, Eastern had sent me a letter saying that "due to your personal leave . . . your corporate active-service date, pay-progression date and date for vacation and retirement benefits have been changed [accordingly]." ALPA's contract with Eastern specified that a pilot could take up to 90 days personal leave with the company's written permission. No such document existed in my case, and the duration of my grounding vastly exceeded the permitted length of personal leave. Yet the company used this ploy to attempt to undermine my seniority. The arbiter dismissed this claim also.

The arbiter ultimately found that Eastern had acted improperly in disciplining me. Eastern had grounded me for medical reasons, he said, and then put me on nonpay status before I could be examined by their doctors. Since I had been subsequently examined by Eastern's doctors and found fit to fly, the arbiter ordered me reinstated, ordered the company to pay me nearly a year's back pay (for the period from June 27, 1977, to June 12, 1978), and he ordered that my seniority, vacation time, and retirement benefits be restored as well.

I wasn't completely satisfied, however. In the year that I was grounded, Eastern had used every trick in the book to break my spirit. On one occasion, when my ex-wife and I were embroiled in a legal battle over the custody of our children, my ex-wife's attorney produced Tom Buttion, Eastern's vice president for flight operations (who succeeded Krepling), who testified as to my alleged mental problems. Buttion's allegations had an adverse effect on the judge's custody ruling.

Later, when the System Board awarded me the back pay for my month-long suspension in January 1977, Tom Buttion called my ex-wife's attorney to inform him of that development. The attorney immediately went into court and got a judgment to take that money for back legal fees. I was depending on that money to pay my overdue bills. As a result of the judgment, my local bank foreclosed on the mortgage to my house.

In June 1978, I filed a $12 million lawsuit against Eastern charging Frank Borman, Tom Buttion, and Bill Bell, Eastern's attorney, with "civil conspiracy to force me out of employment." I felt that I had been vindicated, both by my civil-suit victory and the findings of the System Board. Every charge Eastern had ever made against me was found, by an appropriate authority, to be baseless. Florida law provides that if a group of people who have an economic advantage over an individual come together to use that advantage against that person, a civil conspiracy is created that is a cause of action. If that description doesn't apply to what Eastern did to me, then I don't know what does.

Through a series of complex legal maneuvers, Eastern had the suit moved from the Florida courts to the Federal district court. My employment as a pilot comes under the jurisdiction of the Railway Labor Act. As a result, a federal court will have to determine the applicability of Florida law in my case.

I had thought that my reinstatement and my second lawsuit against Eastern would make the company wary of treating me in the high-handed manner they were accustomed to using. Shortly after I began flying again, I discovered how wrong I was. In October 1978, I was contacted by David Blundy, a Washington correspondent for the highly respected newspaper *The Sunday Times of London.* Blundy had heard about the $1.6 million judgment I won against Eastern, and he wanted to write a story about it.

A month later, on November 19, 1978, the *Times of London* ran Blundy's story—it was titled " 'That Pilot is Paranoid.' " The story went on to quote Jim Ashlock, director of news for Eastern. "Gellert has been complaining for years," Blundy quoted Ashlock as saying. "He said Eastern was out to get him, that we tried to crash a plane in order to kill him, that we deliberately altered the altitude instruments on a plane he was flying. He's paranoid." Astonished by the statement, Blundy went on to ask Ashlock: "Why do you let him fly your passenger jets?" "It's awfully hard to fire anyone these days," Ashlock replied. "Anyway, we have three of them in the cockpit. Know what I mean?"

In a December 1, 1978, letter to the *Times of London,* Robert Christian, Ashlock's boss at Eastern, said that Ashlock denied ever telling Blundy that I was "paranoid." "In fact," Christian stated, "Mr. Gellert has been found to be psychiatrically normal and fully qualified to operate an aircraft in the service of Eastern Airlines." Blundy stood by his story, and the *Times of London* refused to print the retraction that Christian demanded in his letter. In January 1979, I filed a $1 million libel suit against Eastern. In the suit, which is scheduled to be heard in February 1980, David Blundy will appear to testify on my behalf.

Eastern's conduct with the *Times of London* is all too typical of their actions toward me over the past seven years. Ashlock, a professional public-relations executive, was contacted by a reporter for one of the world's leading newspapers. He granted an interview without restrictions, and said something that every first-year journalism student knows is libelous. Suddenly, Eastern is charging that Blundy and the *Times of London* are making up stories, even though both Blundy and Ashlock testified under oath in pretrial depositions that Ashlock made the statements attributed to him. In fact, Bill Bell even went so far in an April 20, 1979, deposition to say that if Ashlock called me "paranoid" in his interview with the *Times of London,* then he committed libel. Bell went on to say that the article also libeled Eastern by implying that the airline would intentionally use a pilot who was paranoid. Yet Ashlock is still employed by Eastern as its news director.

I think there is a great deal of irony here. Airline safety involves more than just correcting specific defects like the L-1011 autopilot. Safety is an attitude which, ideally, should be shared throughout a company from top to bottom. But if Frank Borman and his legal department are consumed with pursuing a vendetta against me, then they aren't dealing with safety problems. Instead, their behavior forces me to fly their planes and their passengers without adequate rest. They publicly label me "paranoid," and yet I'm still flying for them. It doesn't make sense.

I see Frank Borman quite frequently. He is an energetic executive, and our paths have often crossed at airports around the country. In fact, Borman has even flown on several of my flights in the past year— apparently any alleged medical problems I may have aren't enough to cause the former astronaut to avoid flying on my plane.

I ran into Frank Borman on three occasions shortly before I was grounded in 1977. Each time he'd greet me very amicably, slap me on the back, and ask how I was. Then, invariably, Borman would ask, "Did we settle that court case yet?" The first two times Borman asked that question, I replied with a simple, "No." The third time he asked, I couldn't hold back. I said, "Colonel, when that court case is settled, you'll be the first to know because you will have to settle it."

Perhaps that's the greatest irony in my seven-year struggle with Eastern. People look at the record of my fight against the airline, and they tell me, "You've won. You're a winner." I'm not so sure. What chance does an individual have against a $2 billion company that is willing to spend any amount to beat one of its employees?

The last few years have been hard on me. I'm flying again now, but I find that my relations with my fellow employees have changed dramatically. Eastern employs thousands of people. The small percentage of that number who have flown with me know the dishonesty of the company's attempts to discredit me. But the Eastern employees who don't know me personally can't make subjective judgments. I find that many of them try to avoid working on my trips because they've heard that "the company is down on me"—in other words, if something happens on my airplane, they're going to be in trouble because Eastern is going to use every opportunity to get at me.

Eastern's subtle harassment of me hasn't changed either. Recently, I took my first day of real sick leave in years, and I was immediately called into the chief pilot's office to account for myself. I don't especially want to be dragged through an endless series of grievance proceedings again, even though I'm within my rights under the ALPA contract to take sick leave when I feel ill. So if I haven't been allowed to get enough rest, or if I have a head cold and my ears are plugged up, I don't make an issue over it. I just fly.

# Reporting Illegal Campaign Contributions

## Joseph Rose

I began my employment with Associated Milk
Producers Inc. (AMPI) in April 1973, shortly after
my 35th birthday. A 1977 *Wall Street Journal* article
characterized me at that stage of my life as "a young
attorney well on the way to corporate success." I
was unaware, however, that my short-lived
association with the nation's largest milk cooperative
would take me before the Senate Select Committee
on Watergate, the Watergate grand jury and other
grand juries, and nearly ruin my career and my
family.

I was hired by AMPI to be an in-house counsel.
My duties included the auditing and payment of
legal expenses, and the coordination of outside legal
counsel in matters other than antitrust. As an
in-house attorney, I believed that I had certain
obligations to the farmers who were either members
of AMPI or were served by AMPI. They occupied
the same position as stockholders in a major
corporation. They depended solely upon AMPI
management and the cooperative's elected board of
directors to manage their financial affairs and to give

them a truthful, complete accounting of what happened to their money.

I came to AMPI with seven years of experience as a corporate attorney in a series of jobs that gave me a strong grounding in business ethics. From 1966 to 1970 I worked as a civilian attorney for the United States Air Force at Kelly Air Force Base in San Antonio, Texas. My job, which dealt primarily with labor and equal opportunity problems, involved serving as a "prosecuting attorney" against civilian employees who engaged in a breach of ethics, a breach of regulations, or a breach of the law. In 1970 I joined the Gates Rubber Co. in Denver, Colorado, as a labor relations attorney. Gates Rubber management maintained a commendable ethical code, and not once during the years I worked there was I asked to conceal or defend a corporate criminal activity.

I left Gates Rubber to take a job with Montgomery Ward and Company as regional labor attorney for the western part of the United States. Shortly after taking this job, my wife suffered a series of heart attacks, and I moved her and our five small children to San Antonio where relatives could look after her properly. Because of my wife's precarious health, I decided to look for a job in San Antonio. Through the law school I attended, I was put in touch with AMPI and interviewed by AMPI officials early in 1973.

AMPI was at the center of a facet of the Watergate scandal that became known simply as "the milk deal." AMPI, along with smaller dairy cooperatives, made a series of illegal corporate contributions to Richard Nixon's 1972 reelection campaign—estimates of the magnitude of these contributions range from $325,000 to $2 million. In exchange, investigators later charged, President Nixon raised the level of federal milk-price supports for the dairy industry, a favor which Harold Nelson, then AMPI general manager, estimated at the time to be worth $300 million to the nation's milk producers. AMPI and the other cooperatives also made a series of illegal contributions totaling $185,000 to the abortive 1971–1972 presidential campaign of Wilbur Mills, then Chairman of the House Ways and Means Committee, in a similar effort to raise federal price ceilings.

I became aware that something was rotten at AMPI my first day on the job. I was asked to lunch by Stuart Russell, an Oklahoma City attorney who was a long-time outside counsel to AMPI. Russell mentioned a pending antitrust suit against AMPI, and in the course of our discussion he suggested that the cooperative offer a witness in the case a job in order to get him to "clarify" his testimony. I was horrified at the suggestion.

Several weeks later—shortly after the televised Senate Watergate Hearings, which began on May 17, 1973, became a subject of intense interest to senior AMPI executives—I had an opportunity to meet with George Mehren, AMPI's general manager and chief executive officer. I asked Mehren why a man like Stuart Russell was kept on the payroll. Mehren explained that Harold Nelson, his predecessor, had run a "completely corrupt operation," using corporate monies for political campaign contributions. Mehren said that he had put a stop to such activity when he took over from Nelson, but he told me, "We have to keep Russell [on the payroll] as long as the antitrust litigation is going on because he knows where all the dead bodies are."

I was appalled at Mehren's matter-of-fact admission about AMPI's illegal activity, and I was especially bothered that he and other senior executives were doing nothing to recoup monies illegally expended. Their attitude was to remain quiet about these crimes until the statute of limitations on them ran out. One of the main methods for the illegal contributions, I soon discovered, was deliberate overpayments made to some of AMPI's outside attorneys—Russell among them—who would then return some of the money to AMPI officials for political use. I began gathering what evidence was available to me of these overpayments. This was mainly photocopies of checks, including one payment of $66,000 Russell received after Mehren became general manager, apparently to pay income taxes on money that had previously been laundered through him. At the same time, I argued with AMPI executives that they had a legal obligation as well as an obligation to their farmer members to seek the return of the illegal contributions.

As I've previously mentioned, one of my duties at AMPI was to approve payments to outside attorneys. After several months on the job, I began to suspect that some of the outside attorneys were still being used to launder money, and I thought that I might be implicating myself in the crime if I approved some payments I was given. I contacted John Butterbrodt, a Wisconsin dairy farmer who was then AMPI's president, and told him that I wouldn't approve the payments. He laughed at my statement and replied, "How do you know that you are not already implicated, because you do not know what you have signed." At that point, the vague fears I had felt about working for AMPI crystallized into a single, overwhelming fear: I was scared to death.

I decided to contact the FBI. I had worked closely with the bureau when I was employed by the Air Force, and I felt I had an obligation to alert them to what I considered to be serious ongoing criminal activity. At the same time, I strictly limited what I told the FBI because I felt that the information in my possession might be protected by attorney-client confidentiality.

The only other avenue open to me in my effort to correct AMPI's illegal activities was the cooperative's 51-member board of directors. The annual week-long AMPI board-of-directors meeting was held in Minneapolis in 1973, and I flew north in the last week of August in an attempt to alert the board to how their money had been spent. There are certain events that I vividly recall from that week in Minneapolis. I remember phoning my wife long-distance to assure her that, while I'd been prevented from presenting my evidence before the full board, seven directors did come to my hotel room to listen to what I had to say. I remember my frustration and utter exasperation at not being able to meet with the full board or even to find out if the directors I had spoken with had brought up the subject of my charges. And I remember, after nearly a full week of effort, the total sense of failure I felt.

As I was leaving Minneapolis—the day before the start of the Labor Day weekend—George Mehren told me that he wanted to see me in his office on Tuesday, the next working day. I knew why he wanted to see me. Before I left for Minneapolis, I told my private secretary that she would probably never see me again. That prediction turned out to be remarkably accurate. Visiting my office over the holiday weekend, I found a guard posted at the door who informed me that the locks were changed. Obviously, once alerted to how far I was prepared to go with my concern about illegal activity, management decided to prevent me from retrieving any further documentary evidence from my office files. On Tuesday, I came to work and was handed a tersely worded note from Mehren, firing me on the spot for "failure to perform my assigned duties." To this date, no one has ever explained to me what that phrase means.

AMPI immediately attempted to discredit me following my discharge. John Butterbrodt called my home shortly after my dismissal. I was out job hunting at the time and received only the message that Butterbrodt had called. By this time, I realized that I needed witnesses and documentation in any further dealings with AMPI officials. I returned Butterbrodt's call from my attorney's office with him listening in on an extension phone. Butterbrodt wanted to know why I had attempted to go over his head with my charges to the AMPI board of directors. I told him without hesitation that he and other management officials were well aware of my information and had refused to act on the matter. I told him that I thought their punitive firing of me for trying to bring information about misuse of funds to the board of directors was thoroughly improper.

Butterbrodt acknowledged in the phone call that he was aware of previous criminal activity. He later testified that he was aware of the contributions even before I had been hired as the cooperative's in-house counsel. In an apparent attempt to satisfy at least part of my grievance, Butterbrodt asked if I would be satisfied to meet with the executive committee of the AMPI board to discuss my charges. It was obvious to me at this point that discussing the problem with a small clique would be ineffective—a suspicion later confirmed at the trial of Stuart Russell when Harold Nelson testified that the board knew of the overpayments to attorneys about which I wanted to inform them.

Nevertheless, since I felt an attorney's obligation is to his client, I did meet with some AMPI board members when they came to San Antonio a few weeks later—with my own attorney present. I presented the evidence I had in my possession, and I tried to convince them that AMPI had an obligation to recoup the illegally expended funds. I tried to bolster my credibility with these board members by telling them about my spotless employment history, giving them chapter and verse on whom I had worked for, and the excellent character references I had been given over the years. As it turned out, that proved to be a serious error.

I'm convinced now that, under the guise of seeking to inform themselves about my allegations, these AMPI board members—fearing my credibility as a witness because of my excellent past record—were merely trying to gather information to discredit me. Their subsequent campaign included at least one derogatory phone call to an ex-employer —the legal department of the Gates Rubber Co. In another instance, AMPI made derogatory statements about me to a lawyer involved in an antitrust case against them. Both of these attorneys, who were personally acquainted with me, contacted me immediately after hearing AMPI's slurs and described just how my former employers were trying to smear me.

The reasons for the attacks on my character became evident several weeks after I was fired when I was contacted by both the Watergate Special Prosecutor's Office and the Senate Select Committee to testify about AMPI's illegal campaign contributions. My initial reaction, because of my attorney-client relationship with AMPI, was to contact the cooperative's lawyers, telling them the exact dates and times I was to appear. They did not respond to my message, nor did they seek to be represented before either the Senate Select Committee or the Watergate grand jury. I raised the matter of attorney-client privilege before the committee, the grand jury, and before a federal court in Kansas City where I was subpoenaed to testify in the antitrust case. In each instance my claim of privilege was overruled, and I testified to my knowledge about AMPI's illegal activity. One former staff member of the Senate Select Committee told the *Wall Street Journal* that my testimony was a "catalyst." "He was testifying basically to rumors," the staffer said, "but he named enough people to give us all the leads we needed to crack the thing."

The ironic element in that statement is that because of my role in exposing AMPI's illegal actions in the "milk deal," I have been labeled a whistle blower. I never set out to be a whistle blower; I merely tried to alert the appropriate officials at AMPI to the misconduct I became aware of—I felt that was my duty as AMPI's in-house counsel. Even though AMPI fired me abruptly for attempting to discharge my duty, and despite their campaign to discredit me after I was fired, my personal set of ethics dictated that I attempt to shield the company because of the unsettled question of our attorney-client relationship. If I was a whistle blower, I became one reluctantly.

Even though I was a reluctant whistle blower, I paid a heavy price for it. AMPI's campaign against me had its effect: my finances dwindled away; I had to give up my house and move my family into a small and inadequate apartment; and my wife had to go back to work to help support us, even though her health was still delicate. Our family meals consisted of cheap basics like salads, corn bread, and pinto beans. We received anonymous, threatening phone calls, and even my father, who was dying of emphysema, received derogatory calls about me. My father passed away during this period, going to his grave believing that my career had been irreversibly destroyed.

The only break I had after months of job hunting was an offer to practice law with a small firm in west Texas. I went there alone to take the job—at a much reduced salary from what I had been earning—but after a short time the firm dissolved and I was thrown back into the job market. Through the subsequent months of unemployment, I remember praying daily for the help of the Lord, which I believed was the only thing that could salvage my shattered career and help get my family on its feet again. It wasn't until August 1975—nearly two years after I was fired by AMPI—that I obtained a decent job, with the National Treasury Employees Union in Washington, D.C. I owe a permanent debt of gratitude to Bob Tobias, general counsel to the union, Tom Angelo, associate general counsel, and Vince Connery, the union's president, for giving me the opportunity to rebuild my reputation during the year that I worked with them in Washington.

After leaving the National Treasury Employees Union, I got a part-time job teaching law at the University of Texas in San Antonio, and I also began practicing law in a small but respected firm there. Ironically, shortly after I returned to Texas, the last grand jury investigating AMPI's illegal political contributions closed, eliminating my obligation to testify about my knowledge of AMPI for the first time in three years.

Today, I continue to practice law in San Antonio. In my practice, I represent a large number of insurance companies, corporations, and other business interests. I've found clients much easier to come by ever since the *Wall Street Journal* published, in November 1977, an account of my ordeal. The article gave my peers, friends, and associates a fairly accurate view of what happened to me and my family because of Watergate, and that went a long way toward restoring my good name. But November 1977 is a long time from September 1973.

Enough time has passed so that I can honestly say that I no longer hold any animosity toward those officials at AMPI who tried to ruin my career and damage my family's well-being. I certainly don't feel that every corporation is the morass of corruption that I encountered at AMPI. For the record:

- Harold Nelson pleaded guilty to charges related to AMPI's illegal political contributions and was sentenced to a term in federal prison.
- Stuart Russell was convicted on similar charges, but died while appealing his case.
- AMPI itself pleaded guilty to making illegal campaign contributions and was fined $35,000.
- In addition, because of its admission of illegal political contributions, the Internal Revenue Service retroactively revoked AMPI's tax-exempt status and assessed the cooperative $2.9 million in back taxes for the years in question.

There is one final footnote to this whole affair which I suppose one could call my complete vindication. AMPI recently filed suit against Harold Nelson in San Antonio, alleging in their suit precisely the same things that I, as their in-house counsel, alleged and tried to point out to the board of directors. Nelson countersued, charging that the board of directors knew of these criminal activities all the time they were going on, and thus was not entitled to recover their losses from him. He also asked for damages because AMPI wrongfully fired him despite the seven-year, $100,000 per year contract of employment he had with the company. In February of 1980, the Texas court awarded Nelson $1 million. The jury found that a majority of AMPI's directors not only had knowledge of but approved the illegal payments, and therefore had no proper basis for cancelling Nelson's contract on the ground that he engaged in those illegal actions. That jury verdict established just what I had said all along.

# Exposing Risks of Nuclear Disaster

## Peter Faulkner

In 1974 I was working for the Nuclear Services
Corporation (NSC) as a systems application engineer
when, through my studies of safety, management,
and reliability problems, I became aware of many
engineering deficiencies in nuclear power systems
that were already on the market. After a period of
indecision about keeping this information to myself
and not jeopardizing my career, I began to draft a
paper critical of the commercial nuclear industry. On
March 12, 1974, I presented this paper to a U.S.
Senate subcommittee. Three weeks later, I was fired
from my job. I then forwarded to several
government agencies copies of confidential,
proprietary industry documents, owned by the
Edison Electric Institute (EEI), that confirmed many
of the mechanical problems and design inadequacies
in nuclear power systems I identified in my Senate
paper. I also released confidential memoranda by
Paul Dragoumis, then vice-president of the Potomac
Electric Power Company's (PEPCO) nuclear
engineering and construction group, who identified
potentially dangerous design defects in General
Electric reactor containments.

39

As I expected, my engineering career ended abruptly. None of these acts would have been necessary if design inadequacies and defects had been fewer or less severe, or if government and industry had devoted primary efforts toward solving them instead of promoting nuclear technology. I decided that they were necessary in 1974 because public safety was being compromised by the nuclear industry and I am still of this opinion. This conviction compelled me to warn other citizens and the federal government about industry problems. When the government failed to take action I began to realize that, instead of being part of the solution, it was part of the problem.

Shortly afterwards, the industry succeeded to some extent in suppressing the charges and documentary evidence I had tried to bring forward. The government took no action regarding my Senate paper and the controversy died down for awhile. However, other engineers and scientists have since made similar accusations and the industry is now suffering the consequences. Specifically, several plants were shut down, most notably Humboldt Bay, Indian Point 1, and Dresden 1, and others have experienced extended outages; construction and operating permits have been delayed indefinitely; and the industry's worst accident to date —the March 1979 partial meltdown at the Three Mile Island (TMI) nuclear plant—has seriously undermined public confidence in nuclear power. Seven months later, the Report of the President's Commission on the Accident (also known as the Kemeny Commission Report) concluded that the TMI plant was not equipped with adequate safety apparatus, its operators were poorly trained, its emergency procedures were defective, and its control room was not set up to cope with a major emergency. The Commission found that the Nuclear Regulatory Commission (NRC), when called upon to manage the crisis, performed with "marked ineptitude." The Report's summary judgment was: "With its present organization, staff and attitudes, the NRC is unable to fulfill its responsibility for providing an acceptable level of safety for a nuclear power plant." Unfortunately, there are many nuclear plants with problems similar to TMI's and the government's difficulties in coping with the emergency is symptomatic of several deeper problems.

My concern regarding the legitimacy of nuclear power reached a peak more than five years before the TMI accident. This concern arose from firsthand experience at five nuclear plants where I served as a consulting engineer. By the time I was assigned to PEPCO in late 1973, I began to realize the extent to which many safety and reliability problems in nuclear systems derived from overconfident engineering, the failure to test nuclear systems fully in intermediate stages, and competitive pressures that forced reactor manufacturers to market their systems before serious design problems were resolved. (The industry's standard practice was "sell first, test later.") A case in point involved General Electric's (GE) Mark III containment design concept. The Paul Dragoumis memoranda mentioned earlier described three serious design problems in the Mark III system that were still under negotiation two years after the concept was released for marketing. The design problems raised serious questions about the integrity of General Electric's entire product line. I was concerned that a reasonable doubt existed about the safety of over 40 plants in and outside of the United States. In particular, I was worried that workers at the communities near power stations using the Mark III containment might suffer unreasonable risk of radiation exposure. Gradually, I came to realize that a combination of greed and poor planning by government and industry caused unacceptable delays in essential reactor prototype tests. One result of these delays was that the upgrading of safety standards came too late to benefit plants already built. In other cases, plants under construction or on line had to be redesigned; often, expensive components or entire systems had to be torn down and rebuilt. Some deficiencies did not become known until plants were already operating.

Just as I was beginning to doubt the adequacy of the industry's safety controls, I also came to realize that both employer and client expected me to keep these doubts to myself, despite documentary evidence. The rationale for doing so seemed reasonable at the time. The industry was just beginning to mature; plants had not been on line long enough to provide enough data for harsh judgments; bugs were being worked out; and nuclear industry people were learning as they went along. In short, everyone seemed to be doing the best job possible under the circumstances. Why should I take the chance of throwing away my engineering career in a promising field?

There were many reasons why I decided to "blow the whistle" on my employers and the industry as a whole. First, electric generation by nuclear fission involves a technology with an unprecedented capacity for environmental and human damage. Second, I was convinced that there really was a better way to build nuclear plants and that third-party inspection of systems and components—essential to their safe operation —was conspicuously missing from the nuclear industry's quality assurance programs. Third, I was sure that if I presented my criticisms to several agencies at once, I would get a fair hearing; my proposals would not be covered up, and I would either force the industry to implement some long-overdue reforms or would convince the public that the industry was so badly managed that a major reactor accident was imminent. Finally, and most important, I had overwhelming evidence that many nuclear systems were sold before they were properly designed—a practice that carried these systems through the entire construction phase, and sometimes into operation, with unresolved technical questions.

I spoke to many of my fellow engineers and shared their observations and opinions on the industry in an attempt to be sure that I was not merely being a gadfly and that I was indeed defining the problem properly and raising pertinent questions. But although many of my colleagues with far more civilian nuclear experience than I were well aware of the abysmal industry management, I began to realize that they had no desire to "rock the boat." They moved from one day to the next with a benign optimism. The general feeling was that the industry eventually would solve most of these problems and that line engineers should leave complex management and policy problems to executives and experts. It began to appear that I was working with people who had long since accepted their roles as narrow specialists; this perception allowed them to shrug off any responsibility for nuclear industry management problems, even though they saw more clearly than most the hazards posed by inadequate design and testing. Meanwhile, the industry was suffering chronic delays and shutdowns, which created a potentially infinite demand for our services as consulting engineers. I found the inherent conflict of interest intolerable; the awesome safety implications demanded that someone identify and propose solutions for management deficiencies, even though doing so might eliminate future demand for his services.

A small group of us designed a pilot management information system to secure a better degree of quality assurance for our clients and to consider management problems at a deeper level. When this was rejected and when I was told by several senior engineers that our clients didn't want management advice—only technical assistance to get them over the next hill—it occurred to me that no one wanted to explore or remedy the underlying problems.

LATE IN 1973, I asked my superior, Dr. Harry Lawroski, NSC's environmental systems manager and then treasurer of the American Nuclear Society, to help me prepare a paper for publication by the Institute of Environmental Sciences (IES). The paper's abstract emphasized that the nuclear industry had allowed its management philosophy to lag behind its technical development and it proposed centralizing certain functions such as contract negotiation and quality assurance enforcement. Dr. Lawroski approved the abstract in October 1973, and IES accepted it. The initial draft was developed on my own time in November, after I had been assigned by NSC to the Potomac Electric Power Company in Washington, D.C., to assist Paul Dragoumis and Russell Brown with developing PEPCO's comprehensive quality assurance/management information system for the Douglas Point nuclear station.

Two weeks after arriving in Washington, I contacted John Tunney, who at that time was a Senator from California and also a friend from my college and Air Force days. Before running for Congress, John had been my personal attorney, but this time I was the one who was offering advice. I warned John that he should familiarize himself with nuclear industry problems, since they would soon be potent political issues, and I indicated that I would be glad to give him my views. John invited me to meet with two of his assistants, Dan Jaffe and Bob Feyer. Several meetings later, I started work on a background briefing memo for John based on the IES paper, then in its third draft.

Although both papers recommended reforms, I was beginning to wonder if the real problem was with the people in the nuclear industry. There did not seem to be enough really first-rate engineers and executives like Dragoumis and his staff. I had come to respect them immensely, especially when compared with personnel at other electric power companies. If indeed there was a shortage of able people in the industry, it was unlikely that a few legislative or administrative changes would make much difference. And since large numbers of first-rate technical and management people obviously could not be drafted en masse, perhaps my friends at NSC were right in ignoring what they could not change.

Although I couldn't determine the quality of engineer-executives in the nuclear industry without spending years visiting every U.S. electric power company and related federal agency, I had, by this time, gathered plenty of subjective data on management and technical adequacy. But I did not act on this data until similar allegations by Louis Roddis, then vice chairman of the board of Consolidated Edison of New York, confirmed my suspicions.

Roddis was a 1937 graduate of the U.S. Naval Academy who had a distinguished career in the Navy, including an appointment by Admiral

Hyman Rickover as one of the first site engineers in the nuclear submarine program. After leaving the Navy, Roddis joined Con Ed and became its president while the first nuclear plants in New York—Indian Point Units 1 and 2—were under construction. Roddis showed special concern for issues involving safety, design integrity, and the hazards of balancing investment return against high engineering standards. In November 1972, he made an astonishing speech before the Atomic Industrial Forum (AIF), of which he was president, entitled "Maintaining the Output, or Can We Get There from Here?" Roddis submitted data that nuclear plants were generating electricity at a rate of 20 percent less than what had been promised earlier in environmental impact statements. He called for several reforms and, judging by industry reactions, upset a number of people. Industry observers believe that the AIF speech contributed to forces that "promoted" him to his 1973–74 position—more honorary than functional—of vice chairman of the Con Ed board of directors.

On February 3, 1974, the New York *Times* published a short article based on an interview with Roddis, nearly 17 months after his AIF speech. Roddis repeated his earlier charges and alleged that spot checks of plant performance convinced him that nuclear plant electricity production was still far below expectations. He accused industry executives of publishing misleading plant performance data that depicted nuclear plants as producing far more electricity than they really were. Roddis seemed to be telling the industry that it was being doubly dishonest with the public—in its attempts to refute his own earlier data and conclusions, and in trying to foster citizen support for nuclear power by using irrelevant data that concealed the real state of affairs.

Convinced of Roddis's honesty, I was sure that he would make these allegations a second time only if he were under fire and furious about it. After reading the *Times* article and obtaining a copy of Roddis's 1972 speech, I checked his data and decided that he was right. If the industry was putting pressure on him to recant his earlier conclusions, I had good reason to question the industry leaders' ethics, as well as their managerial and technical competence.

THE LAST PART of the puzzle fell into place a few days later. It was on February 10, 1974, while I was working at PEPCO, that I happened to pick up a copy of a memo, written by Paul Dragoumis, from the PEPCO project manager's desk. It described negotiations between his staff and GE on several serious design problems evident in the billion-dollar

Mark III system he had purchased from GE. The most stunning comment in the memo was: "The design of many contemporary containments, not just Mark III, may be in substantial question."

Paul Dragoumis was no ordinary engineer, and this memorandum, containing complete documentation, gave me special cause for alarm. A fiercely aggressive and technically brilliant young executive (he was then 37) with a leading U.S. power company, Dragoumis was without a doubt one of the nuclear industry's best and brightest. Certainly, such a man would be in line for the presidency of the American Nuclear Society, an electric power company, or both. The memos represented Dragoumis's best judgment on design problems that were not resolved before GE released its design concept for marketing. GE apparently gambled that it could market the Mark III, that all technical problems were solvable, and that all would be ironed out in later negotiations between GE and its customers.

I decided soon after that the public should know about this and that I would distribute copies of Dragoumis's memos without his knowledge or permission. If Dragoumis was right, then public safety took precedence over all other considerations—his career and mine, PEPCO's plans to build a plant, industry profits, and adequate electric supply for the country. For what his memos showed beyond a doubt were that serious design defects existed in GE's product line and that GE had rushed its containment design to market before any large-scale prototype tests were run. This amounted to a serious breach of engineering ethics. It also obliged purchasers to become involved in the testing phase, including design verification, prototype, data analysis and, in this case, redesign of the initial concept. The ethics breach turned on the fact that this involvement also imposed a difficult dilemma as well as potential financial losses on purchasers of GE systems if any of these postponed tests yielded problems too difficult to solve. For if any of these problems—Anticipated Transient Without SCRAM (ATWS), for example—were identified as essentially unsolvable after hundreds of millions of dollars were invested, fiscal considerations would weigh heavily in any decision to shut down the project. The momentum at that point would favor going ahead and accepting the risk.

My decision to leak Dragoumis's memos reflected a personal value judgment that, in view of the enormous health hazard, this method of dealing with risks was not acceptable, that it had been going on for years in the nuclear industry, and that it was time to put a stop to it by selective surgery at the point where risks were metastasizing throughout the design and construction cycles.

At this point I stopped giving the industry that employed me the benefit of the doubt. A great many things that bothered me for months began to fall into place: co-workers' comments that power company management was more often than not either incompetent or unequal to the job of running nuclear plants; the suggestion that electric power company top brass had no idea how different, how much more complex, nuclear plants were compared to fossil-fueled plants. Roddis's implied charge that the industry was cutting corners trying to get nuclear plants sold, licensed, and running at any cost confirmed my interpretation of Dragoumis's report that adequate prototype testing was being conducted *after* nuclear systems were marketed. In the end, Roddis's allegations reinforced and integrated all these fragments into one consistent view. Instead of minimizing their significance, I began to seek confirmation and other evidence of dishonesty and incompetence elsewhere in the industry.

At the same time, I completely rewrote both the Tunney and IES papers, spotlighting Roddis's data as the basis for questioning plant safety and reliability, and, ultimately, the competence of industry leaders. In the papers I discussed Roddis's finding that nuclear plants are generating almost 20 percent less electricity than industry executives promised when they applied for hundreds of construction permits between 1966 and 1972. This meant that, if these electric generation rates continued, it would be necessary to build 20 percent more plants to obtain the amount of electric generating capacity promised earlier. The 20 percent shortfall also indicated to me that safety and reliability were less than adequate.

I also mentioned in the papers that frequent and unexpected breakdowns in plant systems have caused unsatisfactory electricity production. Nuclear plants are breaking down frequently and unexpectedly because they are not built properly in the first place—that goes for plant design, procurement, fabrication, construction, and testing. The most effective guarantee that a plant will be built and operated properly is a rigorous quality assurance program implemented from the earliest design stages throughout the years of plant operation. Quality assurance (QA) during these phases of nuclear plant development is inadequate for a great many reasons. For example, third-party inspection of components and systems is not required. Also, nuclear plant management and staff regard QA with resignation and suspicion. But since quality assurance is required by the federal government, many electric power companies reluctantly go through the motions of hiring outside firms like NSC to write their quality assurance programs, appointing marginal engineers from their own staffs to implement them.

I finished the final drafts of the Tunney and IES papers in mid-February. I then forwarded the IES draft to the Institute for comment and delivered the Tunney paper personally to Bob Feyer. On February 25, he called to thank me and to mention that the Senator did not plan any immediate action. Later, I learned that any senator or congressman proposing legislative reforms based on my paper would have embroiled himself in the type of controversy that could seriously damage a political career. Rather than commiserate with John, I forwarded a copy of my paper to Anthony Z. Roisman, a prominent Washington attorney, who urged me to allow him to include it in the U.S. Senate proceedings. I agreed.

At the end of February I returned to California briefly and showed the IES draft to my superiors. Dr. Lawroski thought it was too strong and told me to rewrite it. On March 6, I flew back to Washington to resume my engineering duties at PEPCO and to wait for Roisman to make his move.

By this time my own position had hardened. What started as a technical paper recommending legislative and management reforms became a deliberate attempt to challenge the nuclear industry from within. I had decided to test Roddis's argument and data by resubmitting them to the public. I wanted to know who pressured him and how they made him angry enough to accuse his colleagues of dishonesty. One way to find out was to publicize a paper using his data—adding my own arguments—and to see if the same thing happened to me. I wanted to find out if the nuclear industry was as dishonest and manipulative as Roddis claimed.

On March 12, 1974, a slightly revised version of the Tunney paper was read into the Senate subcommittee Energy Research and Development Administration hearings record by Tony Roisman. On March 15, my lead engineer recalled me from Washington and explained that several power company executives had telephoned Sherman Naymark, NSC's president, to complain about my Senate paper.

On March 18, I returned to the California home office and met with Naymark. I admitted to having forwarded drafts of the IES paper to the Institute, but pointed out that circulating drafts for comment and officially publishing a paper were two different things. If the data or reasoning seemed to warrant revision, I would change the draft before publication. I also admitted forwarding the other paper to Tunney, with a copy to Roisman. I insisted that the writing of what eventually became the Senate paper, revising it to include Roddis's data, and instructing Roisman to submit it to the Senate committee were acts of a *private citizen,* not those of an employee of NSC.

Naymark argued that I acquired my nuclear industry information while gaining experience as an NSC employee, that the paper was directly related to NSC activities, and that I had been identified by the complaining executives as an employee of NSC. I protested that these executives were defining my authorship differently than I intended and that instead of pressuring my employer, they should have gotten in touch with me personally. I asked who applied pressure on NSC and Naymark told me that Southern California Edison and Northern States Power Company, as well as about ten others, phoned him.

Naymark expressed extreme concern about the Senate paper and became quite upset when I mentioned that I hoped to forward copies of it to other agencies. He led me to believe that if I showed "good faith" by withdrawing the IES paper from publication, he would be grateful. The implication was that pressure on me would cease. I did not realize at the time that he was setting me up for termination. I reluctantly withdrew the IES paper, believing that it would be impossible to get anything approaching what I wanted to say cleared by NSC.

On March 23, Dr. John Turner, NSC's company psychiatrist, interrogated me for four hours. His questions attempted to determine whether some hidden motivations or deep-seated hostility on my part were the basis "for circulating papers that you must have known would be embarrassing to NSC." I replied that this was a simple case of citizen duty transcending personal or employee commitments. On Monday, March 25, I retained Michael Kennedy as my attorney. Early the following week, on April 2, 1974, Naymark fired me on the grounds that my usefulness to the company had ended.

After my dismissal, I sent copies of my Senate paper to the New York *Times,* the *Christian Science Monitor,* several New York investment banking firms, Ralph Nader, the California State Public Utilities Commission, and various senators and congressmen. To bolster my argument, I added copies of a lengthy collection of operating reports from all nuclear plants in the U.S.—gathered by the EEI Prime Movers Committee—and copies of the Dragoumis memoranda, which I copied while at PEPCO. There were several documents of an even more sensitive nature that I withheld and stored in safe deposit boxes. I notified industry leaders that if anything happened to me, my attorney would call a press conference and release them.

I then notified the FBI that after I had voluntarily made my views available to a U.S. Senate subcommittee and I was fired from my job barely three weeks later. This, I told the Bureau, was a violation of Title 18, Section 1505 of the U.S. Code, which protects congressional witnesses from reprisal. Keith Barry of the San Jose FBI office initiated a preliminary investigation. In August 1975, the Department of Justice, alleging that I had not been subpoenaed, instructed Barry to end his investigation. I pointed out to him that the precedent set by the disposition of my case appeared to deny statutory immunity to voluntary witnesses who come forward with important information bearing on public safety. Barry said that I was not protected by the law because I had not appeared physically before the subcommittee but, instead, presented the Senate paper through a third party. I told him that I thought this should make no difference, that the same immunities should apply. I maintained that the only relevant facts were that I presented my views openly and voluntarily, that they were accepted and published in the Senate record, and that I was fired soon after. I felt that immunities were being denied to me on very narrow, technical grounds and that the Department of Justice displayed a curious unwillingness to pursue the matter—an unwillingness that, in my opinion, may have resulted from pressure by the nuclear industry.

While the Department of Justice was considering termination of Barry's investigation in April 1975, the Nuclear Regulatory Commission (NRC) announced one of a different sort—not by an independent agency, but by General Electric's customers and by GE itself into the adequacy of its containment system. The Commission explained that the investigation was triggered by "new" data which related to "previously unidentified" hydrodynamic forces that could develop during reactor operation. Dragoumis's memos show that General Electric learned for the first time about these problems on or before June 1973, and *not* the spring of 1975 as the NRC announcement implies. The memos also confirm that GE explicitly minimized the significance of these problems until prototype tests—delayed more than 18 months after the system was released for marketing—showed that these forces could jeopardize nuclear reactor safety.

The 1975 NRC announcement affected 16 electric power companies with 25 General Electric reactors, and required a thorough review of the design adequacy of these plants on the basis that some twenty dynamic loading conditions were ignored in the original design. These same conditions existed to some degree in all other General Electric containments under negotiation, construction, or fabrication. The potential costs to the power companies and ratepayers for correcting containment deficiencies are substantial. The containment system itself is simply not replaceable with a new and improved model; it forms the envelope surrounding the nuclear steam supply system and thereby is inextricably involved with many other vital systems and structures.

Shortly after the NRC announcement, General Electric appointed Dale Bridenbaugh as manager of the Mark I containment review team. Over a period of months, Dale and two other GE engineers, Greg Minor and Dick Hubbard, considered the serious safety questions that were beginning to emerge. In February 1976, all three of them resigned their jobs and began a series of appearances to educate Congress and the public about nuclear risks. The detailed congressional testimony of the "GE Three" tends to confirm my interpretation of the Dragoumis memos and several allegations regarding inadequate quality assurance that appear in my Senate paper.

Since April 1974, I have applied to sixty-seven U.S. corporations for employment in technical areas. All applications have been rejected. Although I now earn an adequate income as a free-lance lecturer and writer, and teach six months of each year at Stanford University, it seems evident to me that I have been blackballed from corporate employment. But I have no grounds for complaint, for who would hire a man who stole and later distributed his former employer's proprietary documents? I have accepted the termination of my engineering career as the price I must pay for bringing the EEI and Dragoumis documents before the public.

Despite the fact that I was fired from my job, that statutory immunities were denied me, and that I appear to have been blackballed from technical employment, I am very optimistic about the future. In the words of Department of Energy officials, the nuclear industry is "barely alive." (Since the disclosure of the Dragoumis memoranda, General Electric had difficulty selling reactor-containment systems featuring the Mark III design and suffered dozens of postponements and cancellations of earlier orders—including the two reactors ordered by PEPCO for the Douglas Point station.) Partly because of the Three Mile Island accident, a great many people are now skeptical of industry claims that the risks of nuclear power are minimal and that the benefits justify them. Every one of my 1974 allegations has been confirmed by other critics, several of whom have extensive industry and engineering experience. More important, the TMI accident validates many of these charges and bestows a degree of credibility on nuclear critics who for years endured harassment, reprisals, and pejorative labels by the pronuclear establishment. A close reading of the public statements and publications of these critics reveals a great deal of consistency. The interlocking nature of their charges is especially striking because they were made by engineers and scientists representing all three sectors—government, reactor vendors, and electric power companies—and who arrived at their conclusions independently.

The conflict of expert opinions on the matter of safety suggests that debate on this topic is unproductive and that a deeper issue is involved. Such has been suggested by Amory Lovins, a physicist and internationally recognized energy policy analyst, who comments on nuclear technology as follows:

> [U]ltimately its safety is limited not by our care, ingenuity, dedication or wealth . . . but by our inescapable human fallibility; limited not by our good intentions, but by gaps between intention and performance; limited not by our ability to solve problems on paper, but by our inability to translate paper solutions into real events. If this view were correct, it would follow that nuclear safety is not a mere engineering problem that can be solved by sufficient care, but rather a wholly new type of problem that can be solved only by infallible people. Infallible people are not now observable in the nuclear industry or in any other industry.

In this short analysis, Lovins pinpoints what I had dimly perceived —but very keenly felt—during my engineering career: that experts on each side of the nuclear issue disagree because they evaluate human experience in fundamentally different ways. The technological optimists—and I used to be one—are convinced that the major problems afflicting the nuclear industry are soluble and that technical fixes will play an important part in resolving these problems. They have faith in the perfectability of man, and it is a fair question whether this faith has an ideological or rational basis. They believe that a proper integration of humans and well-designed technical systems will compensate, with a generous margin of safety, for the unpredictable, unknown domains —the dark side of human potential that history documents and that technologists tend to dismiss as tractable. Technological skeptics, on the other hand, tend to reject these assumptions out of hand. But because the skeptical position is unlikely to support generous R&D subsidies and deployment of hazardous technologies, and because these are sought after as a means to achieve a growing gross national product, it is regarded by most Americans as faintly subversive until an event like the TMI accident convinces them that a healthy skepticism is their only protection against the hazards of proceeding too fast with imperfectly understood technologies.

Any analysis of the nuclear controversy tends to distill two issues that have occupied much of my time since 1974. The first turns on the question of how safe is safe enough? If nuclear systems have been designed as safely as engineers can make them, we must ask—and attempt to answer—whether this margin of safety is adequate, given the catastrophic effects of a major accident. The nuclear industry insists that the probability of such an accident is infinitesimal, and it is true that backup and redundant systems significantly reduce the chances of an accident. To some extent, these systems may buffer reactor operation from human error as well. But complex systems tend to malfunction for complex reasons and in ways undreamed of by their designers. In the end, it may be that man himself may govern accident probabilities that now appear favorably small because nuclear risks were calculated with primary attention to the *engineering* aspects, about which a great deal is known, rather than to the *human* aspects, about which there remains a great ocean of truth to be discovered.

The second issue concerns the division of labor and responsibility between engineers and executives. I believe that an engineer bears *major* responsibility for the safety of the system he designs, and *partial* responsibility for the way in which these systems are used. During the war years—and our country has faced three major wars in the last 35 years—certain pressures on engineers led to a condition where they abdicated more and more responsibility for safety and usage. These pressures, which carried over into peacetime, focused on getting a system operational as fast as possible. Because many of these systems were designed for direct use by or support of the military, engineers simply could not be bothered with the ethical problems inherent in the fact that their systems were being used to kill and maim soldiers and civilians. The issue turns on the fact that what should be the responsibility of the engineer is, to a major extent, co-opted by corporate executives interested in reducing ethical pressures on engineers in the interests of efficient production. After employing engineers, these executives set policy—more often than not by simply saying nothing—that communicates the idea to line employees that *broad questions of safety and usage are not their responsibility.* Certainly the penalty for disobeying this policy is underlined when an engineer takes matters into his own hands, asks sensitive questions in public, and is fired.

If most engineers have abdicated responsibility for these matters, and if executives have co-opted them, then it is also true that executives have not done a very satisfactory job of discharging these responsibilities. This has happened because the highest levels of most corporations are dominated by sales, marketing, and fiscal specialists rather than by senior engineers. The result is that engineering ethics, as I have defined them, play a small part in executive decisions, whether that decision is to market a reactor with unresolved safety problems or to put another on line when delays cost upwards of $400,000 per day. There have been many instances where management has made a fiscally unprofitable decision that favors public welfare, but these are infrequent and are the exceptions that prove the rule. It should not surprise anyone, then, that an occasional engineer upsets the applecart by assuming responsibility for executive matters that are, in his view, unsatisfactorily discharged. Most likely, he will feel keenly about these matters and decide that these responsibilities for safety and usage weigh upon him simply because no one else seems to be shouldering them. The whistle blower/ex-engineer later becomes interesting to citizens who start to ask who, if anyone, is in charge. At this point, the truly important questions are raised and the whistle blower's significance turns on issues of corporate responsibility rather than loyalty.

My experience has been that most engineers are honest, competent, and dedicated people who accept, as a matter of good manners, constraints on their freedom of speech and their right to question executive decisions. The fact that ethical considerations bear on these constraints does not occur to most of them. This oversight is partly the result of poor design of curricula at the undergraduate level, where courses on ethical problems are neglected in favor of additional, narrow training in specialized upper-division topics. Certainly, corporations have an interest in hiring people who defer questions of policy and broad responsibility to their superiors, and this may partly explain the curriculum defects. What I find most striking is that these executives are seldom the ones called upon to defend nuclear technology before the lay public, even though it is these executives who have lifted safety and usage responsibility from the consciences of line employees. Yet it is most often these line employees who appear in public, representing their company or profession, trying to defend a technology whose ethical implications they do not understand and the responsibility for which they are trying belatedly to recover.

How should the responsibility for safety and usage be shared among executives and engineers? If no one is willing to accept final responsibility, does it follow that everyone ends up sharing the responsibility equally and involuntarily? These questions have bothered me for years. They are important to me because the acts I have admitted to here and for which I have paid dearly derived from a unilateral assumption of responsibility for people I sensed were in danger. If these questions are seriously addressed, one answer emerges fairly easily: since executives are free from the detailed duties of engineering design, testing, and marketing, they should be the ones who have—or who should make—the time to deal with and discharge the responsibilities mentioned here. They are, after all, the leaders as well as the employers. This is not to vindicate the hundreds of thousands of engineers who choose to leave these questions to management. The point I would like to underline is that management must have been aware all these years that line engineers were acting obediently and unquestioningly, partly out of fear for their jobs, and that all line employees responded to these fears because management contrived constraints that created these fears in the first place.

So in the end I am inclined to pin responsibility for the engineer's gradual abdication of responsibility on his employers and, beyond them, on the network of managers and executives who developed and tolerated this abdication. This process occurred in the military and in industries other than nuclear power. But it was especially evident in the latter because so many line employees have come forward in the last ten years to criticize the industry. These employees had nothing to gain and everything to lose by blowing the whistle. And it was their employers who had the most to gain by listening; instead, they did everything in their power to convince the public that the whistle blowers were wrong.

The view of the industry that I now hold is that of an intensely bureaucratic, centralized, and dictatorial directorate of nuclear enthusiasts who used every possible means to deploy nuclear reactors worldwide as fast as possible. These executives and engineers avoided the underlying moral and ethical issues of nuclear power. They point to the irreversible deployment of nuclear reactors as grounds for dismissing vital issues as academic when raised, and for suppressing criticism of their objectives and tactics. My original suspicions of managerial incompetence have given way to an even less charitable view: Nuclear industry leaders dwell in the dark caves of the unconscious, and they scream when they see the light.

# Protesting Sex Discrimination against Women

## Cristine Colt

I am a 35-year-old sales and advertising professional
with some 16 years of related sales, marketing,
public relations, and merchandising experience. My
experience in the field includes five years of selling
advertising space for major publications such as
*Saturday Review* and *Cosmopolitan.* In 1974, I began to
look for a more responsible corporate position that
would lead to management. An advertising sales
placement agency referred me to the Dow Jones
Company, publishers of *Barron's* and the *Wall Street
Journal.* I was assured by the agency that Dow Jones
was a company where I could realize my goals.

During my job interview with Henry Marks,
Dow Jones's director of advertising, I emphasized
my desire to move up to a management position. He
told me that there had never been a woman on the
advertising sales management staff of the *Wall Street
Journal* and that the company wished to correct that
imbalance. Therefore, he added, I had come to the
right place at the right time.

55

Marks sent me to see Bernie Flanagan, advertising director for *Barron's*, the sister publication of the *Wall Street Journal*. Mr. Flanagan agreed to hire me at a salary of $20,000 per year to sell advertising in *Barron's*. Flanagan referred me back to Henry Marks, who told me that Dow Jones's affirmative action program sought to remedy the lack of female managers on the *Wall Street Journal* and that my past record made me an ideal candidate for advancement to management. He promised me that as soon as I had proven my selling ability at *Barron's*—a much tougher selling assignment—I would be transferred to the *Journal* in a management entry level position. Even though I didn't get the management position I sought, I was very happy to go to work for Dow Jones. From what Henry Marks said, it seemed it would only be a matter of time before I was transferred to a more responsible position.

When I reported to work on November 18, 1974, however, I was told that my $20,000 base starting salary had been cut back to $18,000 on a take-it-or-leave-it basis, although Mr. Flanagan, my immediate superior, promised that he would "take care of me" through merit increases and a six-month salary review. Though disappointed by the salary cut, the prospect of promotion to management was a powerful incentive to remain. During the first six months of 1975 I put in an average of 70 hours a week on the job. I devoted entire weekends to study, planning, writing sales and promotional material, and developing sales approaches for each client.

I began getting immediate results. *Barron's* was not considered an appropriate vehicle for travel advertising until I vigorously challenged this perception, significantly increasing *Barron's* travel business. I brought in Pan American Airways for the first time in *Barron's*, and also TWA—an account that was sought after for so long that one manager commented, "I remember the number of man-hours chalked up against that account. Jesus Christ! We could've bought an airplane." And I sold space to several hotels that had never advertised before in *Barron's*.

My assignment also included investment brokerage firms. I signed up the largest—Merrill Lynch—to its biggest contractual commitment to *Barron's* in years, a commitment which I continued to expand. I also developed and proposed a special leisure section for the Friday edition of the *Wall Street Journal*, which, if implemented, would have increased both circulation and ad revenue. I gained the interest and support of Merrill Lynch and its advertising agency, but the idea was rejected unceremoniously by Donald Macdonald, Dow Jones senior vice president, and by Henry Marks. (I was later told that Mr. Macdonald said, "What the hell is that little girl up to?") Ironically, the idea of a leisure section was adopted successfully by the New York *Times.* Soon after, the *Journal* followed the *Times'* lead.

In June of 1975, after seven months of employment, during which I met my sales quota for the year in only *half* a year, I made a formal application for the salary adjustment I had been promised. In my request I mentioned the promise of a transfer to management training on the *Journal.* I had increased my total ad lineage assignment (advertising space is measured in column lines) by 77 percent compared to an overall lineage growth for *Barron's* of five percent. I had also increased the amount of advertising space booked by my accounts by 200 percent over the previous year. I felt I had met Mr. Marks's "productivity" criterion for my promised promotion.

A conference was set up between Mr. Flanagan, myself, and Dow Jones's personnel director in response to my request. The matter of salary was discussed and Mr. Flanagan agreed that I should get a merit increase. He also agreed to release me for a transfer to the *Journal*—a development that greatly pleased me. However, Henry Marks, acting on behalf of his superior Mr. Macdonald, vetoed everything a few days later. I then received a letter of reprimand from Mr. Flanagan taking me to task for seeking a transfer and for contacting the personnel director without his approval—although I did so on the basis of a memo from the personnel director asking for input on career goals and stressing Dow Jones's affirmative action commitment. Despite this written reprimand, my merit salary increase went into effect a few weeks later.

In the months that followed, Mr. Flanagan began to intimidate me verbally and criticize my work. He gave me contradictory orders and assignments which made no sense and which cut into my productivity. Mr. Marks also made a number of bizarre statements and suggestions to me. He once pulled up his trousers in front of me and several others and said, "You have great legs, Cris! I have great legs, too! See?"

I tried to take these things in stride, but I soon began to suffer a series of physical ailments, which I have since learned are symptomatic of severe stress. They included a debilitating spastic colon, dermatitis, severe headaches, muscle tension, and insomnia. Over the years, I've had excellent attendance records at my various jobs. But when illness forced me to take sick days at *Barron's,* my medical absences became the subject of additional written reprimands.

In March 1976, I received written notice to attend a meeting with Mr. Marks and Mr. Flanagan, which was to be yet another disciplinary procedure. By this point, I had reached my limit. I consulted with my union, the Independent Association of Publishers' Employees (IAPE), and filed a grievance for the refusal to transfer me, the salary cut, and the constant harassment, which had become increasingly severe.

In the grievance proceedings, the company flatly denied I'd originally been offered $20,000, even in the face of written evidence from the placement agency that referred me and a printed insurance form from Dow Jones's own personnel department indicating my original $20,000 salary level. Dow Jones denied the other grievances and discrimination at the *Journal* as well. The union made no further effort to pursue the matter or file for arbitration.

Faced with Dow Jones's intransigence in denying *prima facie* discrimination at the *Journal*—there still is no woman advertising sales manager, and there never has been one—union indifference, and the danger future harassment posed to my health, and to my career, I filed a sex discrimination complaint, in May 1976, with the Equal Employment Opportunity Commission (EEOC) against both the company and the union.

After nearly a year of investigation, the EEOC found (in March 1977) that the *Journal* indeed had no women sales managers, far too few women sales professionals, and was guilty of discrimination against women as a class. It also found against the union for failing to fight discrimination. The EEOC discounted the hurried promotion of the only other woman in my department, Susan Kaplan, to the position of New York Advertising Sales Manager of *Barron's,* since it was not related to the charge and her advancement took place after I had filed my complaint. Ms. Kaplan, although she had been with the company a bit longer than I, had far less advertising sales experience. (She was later to play a significant role in Dow Jones's retaliation against me following the EEOC's findings. By using another woman to deal with me, Dow Jones evidently believed they could mask the odor of discrimination.)

The EEOC failed to prove discrimination against me as an individual, but after examining the EEOC's files through a Freedom of Information Act request, I discovered that the company based its defense upon misleading sales information. In fact, *Barron's* used what they later admitted—as a result of a 1977 U.S. Labor Department investigation—was an "error" in their account assignments and bonus plan arrangement to discount my claim of being one of the top salespeople at the newspaper. Instead, *Barron's* management told the EEOC that I was "immature" and that my claim to being a superior salesperson was "ridiculous." As proof, the company submitted the sales record of another *Barron's* salesperson, Joel Fainman, who, the company informed EEOC, was a top salesperson, and as a result had received bonuses in 1975 nearly twice as large as my own.

That Fainman received the large bonus payments is beyond question. However, what Dow Jones concealed from the EEOC was the fact that the bonus plan, as it was constituted, gave Mr. Fainman a built-in advantage over me of ten to one. It was only through sheer perseverance and hard work that I was able to cut that margin to two to one. Management justified its devaluation of my work by using volume sales figures to measure sales production, rather than measuring percentage growth of individual accounts over the previous year—the only fair method of comparing different assignments.

The bulk of Fainman's sales assignments were financial advisory service ads, which run in the newspaper almost automatically and require very little sales effort. Fainman's assignment in this area was inordinately large and, as a result, he received $13,750 in bonus payments in 1975 compared to an average for the rest of the staff of $2,450. (These facts were confirmed by the 1977 U.S. Labor Department investigation.) By contrast, the percentage growth figure measures how well each salesperson performs regardless of the volume amount of advertising space. Unlike Mr. Fainman, whose high-volume accounts required very little sales effort, I was assigned mostly travel and brokerage accounts, many of which had never advertised in *Barron's* before. Mr. Fainman increased his sales in 1975 by 13 percent; my own sales increase was 77 percent. Nevertheless, the EEOC accepted *Barron's* statements about my performance at face value.

The company cited the written criticism from my manager that came after my request for transfer or promotion. Although I provided the EEOC with a written, point-by-point refutation of each charge, it apparently had little effect. The company denied making any promises to me at hiring, while at the same time admitting to the EEOC that I had been hired on a special, affirmative action budget.

Dow Jones successfully sidestepped the issues enumerated in my EEOC complaint by attacking my ability on the basis of superficial, misleading, and false comparisons, as well as false criticisms. This tactic was successful only because the EEOC did not have the expertise to investigate records and witnesses—the facts and issues were often related to technical, specialized knowledge of sales, marketing, and publishing. The EEOC was unable to consider the implications of the hiring agreement between Mr. Marks and myself—which the company simply denied *in toto*—because their jurisdiction does not cover contracts, even one entered into under an affirmative action program to correct long-standing discrimination.

Following the EEOC's class action determination against Dow

Jones, the company agreed to conciliation under Title VII of the Civil Rights Act of 1964. However, no summary of the proceedings between Dow Jones and the EEOC was made public and no member of the affected class—women—was present during the proceedings. Without mentioning the EEOC's determination, Warren Phillips, Dow Jones's president and chief executive officer, issued a statement in the company newsletter. Phillips wrote that the company remained committed to affirmative action and would increase its efforts in that area, since there was still progress to be made. The union refused conciliation and the EEOC issued me a Right-to-Sue Letter, which I did not use, because I believed that the company's conciliation would serve my call for constructive change. Unfortunately, I was wrong.

The attitude of *Barron's* management became more openly hostile toward me following the EEOC determination. Early in 1977, several large and lucrative travel accounts were arbitrarily taken from me by Mr. Flanagan and given to Mr. Fainman, who had no prior travel account experience or responsibility. This transfer deprived me of nearly $1,400 in bonus earnings and enriched Fainman by at least that much. Far from equalizing sales assignments at *Barron's,* management made things even more unequal—at my expense.

Mr. Flanagan frequently told me during this time that I had no management potential, that as a salesperson I was not even third rate, and that I was a "pain in the ass." Yet during this same period, clients and other Dow Jones managers referred to me as the best representative in the business, and the best salesperson at *Barron's.* Even when, on one occasion, a client praised my talent in Mr. Flanagan's presence, it had no effect upon his open hostility toward me. At other times, he would grudgingly admit I was good, and then reprimand me for my refusal to give up my requests for management training or transfer.

I was assigned to report to New York Manager Susan Kaplan. She took every opportunity to fault my business methods and style. She also kept me running in circles with assignments that contradicted Flanagan's instructions to me. When I asked him about it, he said to do both. My numerous requests for opportunities for management training, even when in response to personnel office Career Development Memo inquiries, were unanswered.

Yet, regardless of his personal opinions, Flanagan did not want to lose one of his best salespersons to a competitive department. He couldn't wear me down, although my health had been seriously damaged by this point. Since intimidation failed to dissuade me, he tried to "cool me out."

In the fall of 1977, Susan Kaplan's "new issues" lineage—a sales category, which like Joel Fainman's financial advisory service category required little, if any, sales effort—mysteriously appeared in my monthly computer sales report for August. When I asked Ms. Kaplan why this additional block of advertising space, or lineage, was credited to my sales record, she told me it was a "mistake" and supposedly ordered it removed. However, after a client luncheon a few days later, Mr. Flanagan told me that I "would make a lot of money this year. You'll do better here than anywhere else."

On October 14, 1977, at a scheduled sales evaluation meeting attended by Mr. Flanagan, Ms. Kaplan, Bill Sullivan, the third manager in the New York office, and myself, I was offered a deal that involved a direct violation of the written rules of the 1977 bonus plan. I was told that Ms. Kaplan's new issues accounts would be credited to me, which would result in my receiving a large amount of extra bonus money at the year's end. When I questioned the propriety of this, the managers kept urging me to take the offer because I would gain extra bonuses. The offer was withdrawn in embarrassment when they realized I wasn't buying it and Flanagan said he would "correct the computer error." I don't know with certainty what the managers' motivation was in making this offer; I can only assume that they were trying to buy my acquiescence to remaining in my position at *Barron's* and to get me to cease requesting both transfer and promotion.

I tape recorded the evaluation meeting in which the payoff proposal was made. I had openly used a tape recorder in earlier meetings, since I wished to be able to refer back to the managers' suggestions and instructions on each of my accounts. The managers apparently were unaware that I was recording this meeting, probably because they expected to see my old, bulkier machine and didn't know I had bought a smaller one to replace it.

Following my refusal to "play ball," management's attitude became more hostile than ever before. Susan Kaplan started giving me written criticisms of my selling methods and I was ignored or snubbed by the other managers. Understandably, this management attitude began to influence the rest of the sales staff. When an "extra" built into the bonus plan was dropped by top management, a rumor circulated among my co-workers that this was because of my criticism of the plan's design —that it was unequally applied, involved "give-aways," and therefore was not an incentive and constituted a waste of budget. The staff was allowed to blame me for the reduction in their incentive bonus, which was completely untrue.

That the ostracism, hostility, and rejection was neither of my own making nor my imagination is made clear by the attitude of the one salesperson, Nancie Lee, a relative newcomer, who had not been involved. She was quite indignant about the unfairness of it, and she didn't understand it at all. She had not only seen Susan Kaplan turn her back on my "Good morning, Sue," but witnessed similar snubbing behavior towards me by the rest of the staff.

I finished the year 1977 as the number one salesperson in *Barron's* New York office in terms of the percentage of growth of display advertising that I brought in. At a January 23, 1978, sales staff luncheon with higher management, Mr. Flanagan called upon me to comment upon my achievement in 1977. When I said I was first in the New York office in terms of percentage growth, Flanagan cut me off by saying, "No, you're not! We'll discuss that later." At a staff meeting later that day, Flanagan announced the sales figures for the largest percentage growth on the staff—my 18 percent, compared to 17 percent for Joel Fainman, who was second. My actual increase would have been 27 percent had I retained the hotel accounts, which were transferred to Fainman earlier in the year. Still, Fainman was pronounced *Barron's* number one New York salesperson because his lineage volume was the largest.

The next day it became obvious to me that management was using my record of achievement to alienate me further from the staff. Austin Le Strange, another salesperson, came over to my desk and became very abusive. He told me that by raising the issue of my percentage growth figure I was acting "like a child." Le Strange, whose percentage growth for 1977 was 13 percent, emphasized his larger sales volume and said to me, "You're not the number one anything. . . . You're bullshit, Cris!"

Meanwhile, the silent treatment by everyone on the staff except Ms. Lee intensified. Finally, on February 12, 1978, I sent a report to Mr. Ray Shaw, the executive vice president of Dow Jones, with whom I had met previously. I informed him of the ostracism and supplied proof of it, reasserted the correctness of my statement at the luncheon, reported on the unfair transfer of the travel lineage, the unfair downgrading of my professional abilities, and the refusal to even discuss training for advancement. My report was couched in conciliatory language and offered several constructive proposals. I pointed out that a year had passed since the conciliation agreement with the EEOC and that the situation at the *Journal* remained unchanged. I asked his advice on how I could best prepare myself for greater responsibility in service to the company. I informed him that I had spent over $1,000 of my own money on the American Management Association's at-home Certificate of

Business Management Course—AMA's equivalent of an M.B.A. I also reported that my health was being seriously affected by the ostracism and the other forms of harassment. (My physician informed me that severe stress was the root of a painful spastic colon condition which caused me to be incapacitated frequently during early 1978.)

Mr. Shaw did not respond to my report and the ostracism became worse. My health was so badly affected that I was on the verge of exhausting my maximum number of absences under the health plan. Then I learned that Mr. Shaw left on vacation a week after receiving my report and—to the best of my knowledge—assigned no one to follow up on it. I felt I had no alternative but to forward a copy of the report to Warren Phillips, the president and chief executive of Dow Jones. I requested an emergency meeting since the stress caused by the ostracism was destroying my ability to function. I requested that the evidence supporting my charges be given a timely and fair hearing by senior management.

My letter to Mr. Phillips was dated February 20. When I contacted his office on Monday, February 27, I was told he would not see me but had assigned Mr. Shaw to look into the matter. Shaw was scheduled to return on Tuesday, the 28th. Mr. Phillip's administrative assistant told me that an appointment was made for me with Shaw for Wednesday morning March 1, which the personnel manager confirmed. When I arrived for that meeting, I was told that Shaw cancelled it, and I was referred to Mr. Flanagan, the individual I was complaining about. I became physically ill at that point and had to return home and seek medical attention. I immediately wrote to the personnel manager requesting that a union representative be present at any disciplinary meeting with Mr. Flanagan—an employee's right by union contract.

The following day, March 2, I was discharged by Mr. Flanagan by letter, without an explanation or hearing. The reasons for my firing, given to me two weeks later after I made a formal request, were: "overall irresponsible conduct and attitude towards your job as reflected in your refusal to follow instructions, unreliability, excessive absenteeism, tardiness, lack of cooperation, and requests by numerous customers to have you removed from their accounts." No examples of any sort were given and I was denied severance pay.

Following my discharge, I summarized the contents of my February 12 report to Ray Shaw in a report to the company's outside directors, who were in town for the March 15 Annual Stockholders' Meeting. In this document I disclosed for the first time, with transcript, the payoff offer made to me the previous autumn. I called for an investigation of the discrimination, the retaliation, the possible fraud in the bonus plan manipulation and of my discharge—all in the best interests of the stockholders. I asked: "Does not Dow Jones's editorial policy speak out strongly for the fullest hearing of every human rights question? These questions, in this instance ethical as well as economic, will not be silenced by less than the fullest explanation. . . . Therefore I am calling upon you in your capacity as a corporate trustee to move for a resolution of the board to pursue this matter vigorously." I offered to appear before a committee to answer any questions. I received in acknowledgment only the half dozen or so green registered mail return receipts, all dated and signed by the Dow Jones corporate secretary for each of the officers.

After attempting to present my case before the Dow Jones board of directors, I contacted my union, asking it to initiate an investigation. My request was referred to Harry Hochler, chairman of the grievance committee of IAPE. After a thorough investigation of my allegations, Mr. Hochler wrote to union president George Kennedy in July recommending that the union back me completely. Hochler said he was both "surprised" and "embarrassed" that the union previously did so little to protect my rights, especially in light of the EEOC's 1977 finding of discrimination against both Dow Jones and the union.

Mr. Hochler was particularly upset about the manner of my discharge. "The mere naming of charges that are vague and without specifics does not qualify as 'just and sufficient' grounds for discharge," he wrote. "The mere fact of the company's having made such a nebulous charge and repeatedly refusing to back it up with firm evidence or even the names of the complaining parties . . . has the coloration of a sham, particularly in light of [the] countercharge that the firing was set up in retaliation for Ms. Colt's equal rights actions."

Hochler concluded: "I am convinced that the real reason Ms. Colt's manager fired her is because she filed an EEOC action, and the company has been trying to build a case for discharge when she persisted in pursuing her Title VII rights. I have also examined the evidence for her charge that the *Barron's* bonus plan was manipulated to deprive her of rightful bonus earnings and to diminish her performance. I am convinced that the situation calls for an in-depth investigation."

Why did Dow Jones conduct itself in such a manner? I feel that Dow Jones originally hired me as window dressing, so they could point to me as their woman manager-in-training. As long as I did not ask for advancement to a significant managerial post, things probably would have been all right. But when I pressed them for the promotion I felt

I had earned, they turned on me. My case also suggests that the EEOC, in its desire to acquire a "corporate body-count" of findings of discrimination, suppresses individual charges in favor of class action findings. Since class action findings deal in abstractions and not with an individual charging party with specific and clear-cut demands, they are more palatable to the accused company. Conciliations based on such findings have even less force than a consent decree, since there is no actual attempt to monitor or ensure compliance by the guilty company.

Each time a corporation suppresses or avoids an issue like sex discrimination, whether through legal technicalities or public relations, it only wins a pyrrhic victory that subverts the benefits of bettering the "quality of life" at the workplace. Given the inherent weakness of many grievance processes, I think that congressional legislation may be the only way to resolve human rights issues within the corporations—in the absence of a "corporate environment" officer or other ombudsman. Certainly, the grievance process at Dow Jones was inadequate for solving my problem. Having to go through the bureaucratic hierarchy, I was forced to seek redress from the very individuals who were abusing me. When I went over their heads in the company structure, I was summarily fired.

Nevertheless, since my experience involved activity protected under the Civil Rights Act, at least I had the EEOC to serve as the final arbiter. In August of 1978, I filed yet another complaint with that agency —this time for harassment and retaliatory firing as a direct result of my previous EEOC action. I won my first round on August 15, 1978, when New York State Unemployment examiners awarded me unemployment benefits, overriding Dow Jones's objection that I was fired for cause— normally an unbreakable barrier to eligibility.

It seemed to me somewhat vindictive when Dow Jones objected to my applying for New York State Unemployment Insurance benefits, adding to their earlier reasons for firing me the allegation that I had been "insubordinate." The charge of insubordination was not mentioned in the company's official letter to me giving their so-called "just causes" at the time of my dismissal. To be sure, Dow Jones's attempt to block my receiving unemployment insurance caused me much trouble and anxiety. Yet it proved to be a blessing in disguise because it enabled me to present all the basic issues of my unemployment experience to a New York State Administrative Law Judge, and the result of that opportunity was an across-the-board vindication.

The examiner who initially handled my case at the New York State Unemployment Insurance local office was exceptionally capable and was sensitive to my predicament. Mr. George Forsythe, the examiner, listened to my story and carefully considered the evidence. After requiring me to provide additional medical certification from my doctor, and then asking the company for their version of the "final incident" leading to my discharge, he determined that I was indeed entitled to unemployment insurance. The critical issue was the charge of insubordination, since the law judge ruled that my medical absences could not be a disqualifying factor in themselves. When asked to be specific about the precipitating incident, Dow Jones's personnel manager stated in writing to the Unemployment Local Office that on February 27, 1978, while I was in the company president's reception area, "Ms. Colt was then directed by me to report to work which she did not." This was a calculated lie, which backfired when it was made under oath on the witness stand.

The appeal hearing on my request for unemployment insurance was Dow Jones's first chance to parade all of their phantom allegations about my character and performance in public before an impartial hearing officer. As a matter of fact, the case did not require the company to present their entire catalogue of charges because there was only a limited set of issues that were relevant to my receiving unemployment insurance. Nevertheless, they reiterated every charge and in doing so provided me with the opportunity to reply—in a legal forum—to these trumped-up charges.

On the witness stand, Bernie Flanagan, my former manager, asserted that "Cris did not give us sales reports," and "She never accounted for these reports." In fact, the evidence he himself submitted showed that I *did* hand in reports. However, these reports were based on a period when I had been on medical disability for much of the time and therefore was unavailable to make sales calls on which to report. Furthermore, there were other weeks during that period when everyone had been ordered to work as a team on a different type of sales project for which no reports were required. Another example of company misrepresentation at the hearing involved my manager's allegation that my aggressive selling style caused *Barron's* to "lose" a particular client. When I cross-examined him about this claim, he hastily modified his position, saying that he meant that business had only fallen and not that it had been totally lost, and that this was only in one particular year. The sales records show, however, that this client's drop in business was very small, that it was due to internal factors, and that the very next year I got them to increase their advertising in *Barron's*.

Eventually, the hearing focused on the charge of insubordination.

By this time the company had learned—through the grievance sessions with the union—that I had tape-recorded critical events. Thus, in contrast to their unequivocal written statement to the unemployment office, which was the basis of their appeal, their sworn testimony at the hearing became ambiguous and evasive. Nevertheless, they painted a picture of me as an "aggressive," "unreasonable," and "obnoxious" person, who "camped out," "barged in," and "created a disturbance" in the president's reception area, and who disobeyed a direct order to return to work.

I was in a situation in which the company had several witnesses— the personnel manager, the president's secretary, and the executive floor receptionist (all women)—ready to support its case of insubordination. It would have been my word against the testimony of three witnesses easily subjected to company pressure. However, as I noted earlier, I was carrying a tape recorder for normal business note-taking purposes at the meeting in which the three *Barron's* managers tried to buy my good will with the promise of extra bonus money, enabling me to prove that the attempt had been made. After that incident, I carried a tape machine to all business meetings—not just as an electronic note pad, but in defense of my right to work without being harassed and intimidated. These tapes clearly established my version of the events that led to my dismissal and refuted the false testimony by the company's witnesses.

Of course, Dow Jones strenuously objected to the use of taped evidence, incorrectly describing it as "illegal" and equating it with wire tapping. When the judge informed the company's attorney that it was not illegal, the attorney then called it "repugnant." In response to the company's objections, the judge stated: "The general theory in quasi-judicial administrative hearings is that you accept all forms of evidence and that you give them the weight that they are entitled, and the decision must be based upon substantial evidence. . . . And all authorities on administrative hearings say that you should take it into evidence."

After three separate hearings, the judge issued his determination on January 10, 1979. His findings of fact supported me on all the issues of the cause of discharge. I was especially pleased with his finding that I had always operated through "proper management channels. When [Ms. Colt] would be denied a decision promptly at one level, she would appeal to the higher level." In addition, the judge made the following basic points in support of my claim: "She was always performing to the best of her ability. Her conduct did not rise to the level of misconduct and she is not subject to disqualification. . . . When she was absent, she had compelling reason to be absent for illness. The testimony did not prove insubordination. I believe that claimant became dissatisfied with the employer and the employer became dissatisfied with claimant both *because of her filing her EEOC claim* and because she was not advanced at a rate that she considered commensurate with her performance."

Dow Jones appealed the judge's decision to the Review Board, which affirmed the decision, stating that "the administrative law judge's findings of fact and opinion are fully supported by the record." My victory on these issues was especially gratifying, given the amount of evidence marshalled against me, and the array of false charges mustered by the company in defense of its punitive attempt to deprive me of my unemployment insurance benefits.

Shortly before the law judge's decision, I filed a sex discrimination/retaliation complaint against Dow Jones with the New York City Human Rights Commission (qualifying as a joint filing with the EEOC). In addition to the issues of statutory and contractual rights under Title VII and the collective bargaining agreement, I argued for constitutional protection for my appeal to the president and chief executive officer of Dow Jones. I hoped that ultimately a judicial ruling would establish, at least under the circumstances existing in my case, the protection of employees on the job by the Bill of Rights, a protection that one might hope can be extended to include all employees. In my complaint, I argued that I was terminated without due process, in violation of my constitutional rights to freedom of speech, petition, and due process. Furthermore, I maintained that I was terminated in denial of my right to petition peaceably for redress of grievances, which I attempted in my actions to arrange a meeting on February 27, 1976, with Dow Jones President Warren Phillips.

Finally on November 7, 1979, the case was resolved in an out-of-court settlement. While the terms of the agreement do not allow disclosure of the particulars, the outcome goes a long way toward vindicating the rights of an employee in such a situation. There is no doubt that the long battle was draining emotionally and physically. But it also brought the gratification of standing up for what is just and fair. Perhaps, as a result of this experience, some of the people who hold high positions at Dow Jones will rethink their attitudes about how workers should be treated. If nothing else, perhaps the case will inspire someone in a similar situation to fight back when the corporate powers grossly violate human rights in the workplace.

# Resisting Sexual Demands on the Job

## Adrienne Tompkins

Seven years ago I was the victim of sexual
harassment on the job. Unlike many other women
who suffer similar abuse, I did not give in and
refused to leave my job voluntarily. As a result, I
paid a high price financially and in terms of my
health. Ultimately, though, I had the satisfaction of
hearing a federal appeals court judge rule that the
sort of harassment I suffered—which previously was
considered outside the protection of the law—was,
in fact, a form of sex discrimination and a violation
of Title VII of the Civil Rights Act of 1964. This is
the story of how I won my victory.

 I began work at Public Service Electric and Gas
Company in New Jersey in April 1971. In August of
1973 I started working as the private secretary—my
title was "stenographer"—to a new supervisor. On
October 30 my supervisor told me he wanted to
discuss my promotion, over lunch, which surprised
me since I had only been working for him for a
short time.

During this luncheon, at a nearby hotel restaurant, he said he "wanted to lay me" that he "couldn't walk around the office with a hard-on all the time," and that "it was the only way we could have a working relationship." When I tried to leave the restaurant, he restrained me physically, and told me I wasn't going anywhere except with him to the executive suite on the thirteenth floor of the hotel. When I protested again, he advised me not to seek help, saying that he had "something" on everyone in the company, including top management, and no one would help me. This made sense to me, since he held a key position in the company.

I was frightened. I didn't know what would happen if I resisted him, but I felt I had to find a way to maneuver out of it. I recalled being told he had been very close to his late mother, so I mentioned my mother and her recent operation. I told him that she needed me at home and that I was already late for my appointment with her. This apparently moved him enough to allow me to leave, but not before he forcibly held and kissed me.

Initially, I felt I had no alternative but to leave the company. However, I was supporting myself and my mother at the time and I was paying off a large car loan, so I could not take unemployment lightly. I sought advice at my unemployment office and was told that it might be possible to collect benefits when you quit a job because of harassment, but that an investigation would have to be held first. They suggested I first request a transfer through the personnel department, which is what I did.

My supervisor's superior then contacted me and listened to my story. He seemed genuinely concerned, advised me to stay home for a day, and said he would look into the matter. But when he called the next day, his attitude had changed completely. He spoke of "a big misunderstanding" and advised me to return to work. I angrily told him that under no circumstances would I continue to work for the same supervisor and that my unemployment office had informed me that I could file a complaint. He then shifted his position and said a comparable position would be found for me elsewhere in the company. I was very trusting at that time and so I went back to work for Public Service Electric and Gas.

The "comparable" position turned out to be a lower-level one, but I was assured it was only temporary. My duties in this new position were almost nonexistent; I felt as though I were just occupying space. When I noticed and then asked why stenographers were being hired from outside the company, I was told I would be interviewed shortly.

However, the interview I was eventually granted was not for a comparable position. I was asked my reasons for requesting a transfer, and I tactfully said there had been a problem with my former supervisor. Yet when I returned to my department, I was berated for saying too much, was told I was lucky I wasn't being sued for slander, and that I should have been fired long ago!

I realized then that I was not going to be transferred and that the company was going to make things as difficult as possible for me. This was confirmed when I was subsequently informed that no one wanted me because of my frequent absences and my inability to perform my duties. The charges of frequent absences and poor job performance were all fabrications. My absences were not excessive: I had not even used up my paid sick days. As to job performance, my salary and responsibilities increased with each move I made in the two years I worked at the utility, which is a good indication that I was performing my duties properly. I challenged their accusations with these facts.

Once again I contacted my unemployment office. I was told that I could resign and file charges against the company for failing to reinstate me as promised, as well as against my supervisor for harassment. When I told the utility that I intended to do this unless transferred as promised, they granted a transfer to another position not comparable to my previous job. But because I needed the work, I took it.

Shortly after returning to work, the secretary from my former department, which served as the personnel office for that division, told me that a large amount of written material about me was coming in from other departments in which I had worked. Each report said that because of poor job performance I had been transferred out. Looking back, I can only guess that my threat to press charges unless appropriately transferred had prompted the company to amass "evidence" against me. Department heads probably were ordered to forward statements as to my "poor performance." It now became clear to me that nothing had really changed and that my days at the utility were numbered.

I began to get physically ill, suffering a variety of anxiety symptoms such as nausea, palpitations, extremity pain, and occasional fainting spells. My absences were closely monitored and pay deducted from my salary. If notes from my doctor did not meet what seemed to be arbitrary and fluctuating specifications, I again lost a day's pay.

When the situation became so unbearable that I could not bring myself to go to work, I contacted my doctor and asked him to recommend a psychotherapist to help me. After one three-day absence, in July 1974, I was informed that since verbal counseling about absences did no good, I was to receive a disciplinary lay-off of one week without pay. I had never received any "verbal counseling" about absences.

Despite such treatment, I remained at my job, although the harassment continued and my absences became more frequent. With support from my therapist I filed charges with the Equal Employment Opportunity Commission (EEOC), even though they advised me that there were no laws governing sexual harassment. I continued to file additional charges as incidents occurred, hoping a favorable decision would be made while I was still employed. I received a second disciplinary lay-off in August—this time two weeks without pay.

I was fired, finally, in January 1975. The EEOC investigated the company's charge of excessive absence and no cause was found for my charges. The commission did issue me a Notice of Right-to-Sue.

Some people may feel that I could have saved myself a lot of anguish had I just left my job. But I had earned my employment and I wasn't going to let it be taken from me. Others may feel I did all I could. Maybe I did. But it wasn't enough to protect my job. I did not know my rights—or even that I had any in this situation. I lacked a vehicle to deal effectively with my problem. I had been trusting, had followed procedures, and was powerless, given the company's intransigence and duplicity, to get a fair hearing on my charges of harassment.

Disillusioned, I took my Right-to-Sue Notice and filed an affidavit with the federal district court in Newark, asking them to appoint an attorney for me. The court put me in touch with the Women's Rights Litigation Clinic at Rutgers University Law School in Newark, New Jersey. They agreed to represent me, and my case was presented before the United States District Court for the District of New Jersey in 1976. The court upheld my charge against the company but dismissed my charge against my supervisor. In his decision, the judge characterized my experience as a "physical attack motivated by sexual desire on the part of a supervisor and which happened to occur in a corporate corridor rather than a back alley." In other words, the utility had no responsibility for the actions of my supervisor, since it was considered a personal matter.

However, when I appealed my case to the United States Court of Appeals for the Third Circuit, the court noted that the district court's characterizing my supervisor's act as an abuse of authority for personal purposes overlooked the crucial issue. The utility knew about the incident and had not taken immediate and appropriate remedial action. Therefore, the company had acquiesced to my supervisor's sexual demands, making them a necessary condition for continuing in my job.

The setting of the incident—a luncheon to which my supervisor invited me for the sole purpose of discussing my promotion—was strong evidence of a job-related condition, the court said. More important, my supervisor's saying "It's the only way we could have a working relationship" was a clear indication to the court that my employment depended on acceding to his sexual demands. Because my job status depended on agreeing to his demands, my claim fell within the jurisdiction of Title VII, and the court reversed the dismissal of my complaint and remanded the case to the district court for final determination.

By persisting in my lawsuit, I believe I may deter other companies from turning a blind eye to overt sexual harassment on the job—which countless female employees suffer daily. If the courts cannot guarantee women freedom against sexual abuse, then I can only hope that legislation will be enacted to accomplish this end.

But perhaps court-ordered protections will be enough. Remanded to district court, my case was finally settled out of court. Under the terms of a February 1979 court order Public Service Electric and Gas paid me $20,000 for physical and emotional damages, plus my attorney's fees and court costs of over $47,000. Furthermore, under other terms of the settlement, the company had to notify every nonunion employee (about 13,000) in writing about their rights under Title VII. Second, a review panel was set up to hear all grievances regarding sexual harassment, discharge for cause, or any grievance involving job or salary discrimination under Title VII. All review panel meetings are to be recorded on tape for documentation purposes and the panel's decision and reasons for their decision are to be put in writing to the employee. The panel is to consist of an employee of the complainant's choice, an employee at the same job level as that of the complainant, any witnesses, the employee relations manager, the EEOC manager, and the industrial relations manager. Third, a film about discrimination by my attorney, Nadine Taub, and me is being shown on an ongoing basis to all employees at the utility. It illustrates the different types of discrimination covered by Title VII, what protection is available, and what resources are available to an employee who wants to take action. Fourth, a pamphlet entitled "Employee Relations Review Procedure" documenting the steps in processing a complaint is being distributed to every employee and, according to my understanding, has become part of the company's administrative procedure booklet. Finally, my own personal file has been reinstated to what it was prior to the initial incident. Any information released to prospective employers will be limited to the fact that I was employed there and the dates of my employment. If the company violates any of these conditions, it will be held in contempt of court and the case can be reopened.

I was happy about my court victory, but the $20,000 award hardly compensates me for the mental anguish and the months of unemployment that followed my dismissal in January 1975. Immediately after I was fired, I went looking for other office work. But the fact that I could not use Public Service Electric and Gas Company as a reference hindered me and I was unable to find another job. So I decided to go back to school and, in September of 1975, enrolled at Jersey City State College. A year later, while still attending college full time, I began working as an office temporary. In the fall of 1976, I got a permanent position with a company I worked for on a temporary basis. At the same time, I continued my schooling, received my B.A. in communications in June 1978, and I am now looking for work in that field. Reconstructing my life during these last few years has not been easy. But I prefer the pain and sacrifice that come with building a new career to the shame and humiliation I would have felt had I given in to sexual harassment.

# Refusing to Work at Unsafe Construction Sites

## Robert Elliot*

Robert Elliot thought his career had reached a new
plateau when he went to work for the P & Z
Construction Company as a pile-driver foreman in
1975. Following his discharge from the Marine
Corps six years earlier, Elliot had started working his
way up in the heavy construction industry. He
received his pile-driver permit in 1971 and began
working on various jobs connected with the
construction of the Washington, D.C., Metropolitan
Area Transit Authority's massive subway
construction project. Elliot was working regularly
and his skills were in demand.

By September 1975, when P & Z, a California
company, hired him to head one of their pile-driving
crews, Elliot had already worked as a pile-driver
foreman and superintendent at a number of other
jobs—all without incident. Elliot was a hard worker
who received commendations from his employers for

*Written by Albert Robbins

his diligence on the job. To Elliot, P & Z was another step up the ladder. He had no way of knowing that by taking the job he would soon be jeopardizing his career because of his refusal to accept hazardous working conditions without complaint.

Elliot and his crew of pile drivers worked at an outdoor site—an "open cut"—during his first month on the job for P & Z, and the work progressed routinely. Then, in October, Elliot and his crew were transferred to a closed site known as Metro D-1, a subway station under construction at 12th Street and Constitution Avenue, N.W., in the District of Columbia. From the moment he saw Metro D-1, Elliot was appalled by the unsafe conditions at the site. In his six years as a pile driver, Elliot had never encountered such hazardous working conditions. Unguarded 13,000-volt electrical cables ran through the work area. The cables were fully energized and unprotected, except for standard insulation. At other job sites where Elliot had worked, cables such as these either had been disconnected, or they had been sheathed in a protective metal casing so they couldn't be struck accidentally by a pile or burned inadvertently by a welding torch.

The unprotected live cables in the work area, which created a real danger of electrocuting someone, were not the only serious safety hazards at Metro D-1. The work area was littered with large accumulations of combustible trash that could easily have been ignited by a welding torch. The crew was given a mechanically defective crane with which to lift heavy steel beams. And to compound the dangers, both the lighting and the ventilation at the work site were inadequate.

Pile-driving is a dangerous job, even when safety standards are strictly followed. Elliot, who served in the Marine Corps as a platoon leader, felt a similar responsibility towards his crew of pile-drivers, and he was very concerned that P & Z, through its failure to follow recognized safety procedures, was making a hazardous job even more risky. He felt compelled to correct the hazards at Metro D-1.

At the time he went to work for P & Z, Elliot was taking a course in the Occupational Safety and Health Act of 1970 (OSHA), sponsored by the Metro Insurance Administration (MIA) of Washington. Elliot knew that OSHA gave him the right to complain to P & Z about the working conditions at Metro D-1, and that he was protected under Section 11(c) of the act from any retaliation by his employer for seeking to correct unsafe working conditions.

Among other things, Section 11(c) protects workers who complain to their employers about safety and health hazards, discuss safety and health problems with their fellow workers, file grievances concerning safety and health on the job, participate in OSHA inspections, testify before any properly constituted panel about safety and health dangers, and, under certain conditions which have yet to be clarified by the federal courts, refuse to perform a dangerous task. Employees who exercise their OSHA rights are protected under 11(c) from being fired, demoted, or assigned to a less desirable job or shift because of their health- and safety-related actions. Employers are also prohibited from denying sick leave or vacation time to workers because of their OSHA-protected action, from spying on such employees or harassing them, from taking away company housing they may have provided, or from cutting off an employee's credit at banks or credit unions.

Aware of the rights he enjoyed under OSHA, Elliot went to his immediate supervisor, superintendent Leonard Derse, and complained about the hazards at Metro D-1. He also brought the problems to the attention of P & Z's safety superintendent, John Fallon. After several weeks of going through P & Z company channels—with no effect— Elliot decided to take his complaints to outside agencies. Conditions were so hazardous at his job site that Elliot felt that his crew was in imminent danger.

On November 11, 1975, Elliot contacted a representative of MIA and made him aware of the safety hazards that existed at Metro D-1. He also spoke with Nicholas Zampini, an inspector for the National Loss Control Service Corporation, the investigative arm of MIA, who inspected the site. Two days later, Elliot sent his project manager a letter explaining why he had gone to outside agencies to register his complaint; copies of the letter were sent to Roy Huffman, P & Z's general superintendent; John McConnel, the construction superintendent; Derse; the two MIA representatives; and the local business agent for the pile-drivers' union. The next day, November 14, Zampini issued written warnings to P & Z confirming the validity of Elliot's complaints.

Elliot's superiors labeled him a troublemaker and began to look for an excuse to fire him. Management considered any interference on the job site to be money lost, and the fact that Elliot's complaints arose because P & Z didn't follow approved OSHA procedures made little difference to them. Derse, in particular, became overtly hostile to Elliot. Derse told a fellow P & Z supervisor, "All these men want to do is bitch and gripe about safety. They are not interested in working. If I have to go through the entire Washington-Baltimore area, I will find some guy who wants to work and stop bitching about safety."

Elliot's crew of pile drivers supported his efforts to correct the safety conditions at Metro D-1, but they were hesitant to express their support vocally. They shared a "what's-the-use" attitude, convinced that the only outcome of Elliot's actions would be his speedy and forced departure from the job. Only one member of the crew, Patrick Coady, spoke up to management on Elliot's behalf, and he began to receive equally hostile treatment from Derse. Soon, Coady and Elliot were considered a team.

On November 20, 1975, P & Z found an excuse to fire the two troublesome pile drivers at Metro D-1. A member of Elliot's crew, lifting a steel beam from the excavation with the defective crane, dropped the weighty piece of metal, severing one of the live 13,000-volt cables. This, in turn, electrified a steel network beneath 12th Street, N.W. Someone could easily have been killed in the mishap, but, fortunately, the accident occurred just as the lunchbreak was beginning and most of the workers were out of the excavation site.

P & Z fired Elliot and Coady that same day for their alleged part in the accident. The company charged that the accident was caused by unsafe procedures: failing to use tag lines, choking the steel beam on the crane off center, and allowing lacing steel to lie about on the flanges of street-support beams. P & Z had never fired anyone before for involvement in an on-the-job accident. Despite the fact that the company had an internal disciplinary procedure, under which—if the charges against Elliot and Coady were true—they should have received a written warning, they were peremptorily fired. Coady was not even in the excavation hole when the beam fell.

P & Z's case against Elliot and Coady was defective from the outset. Shortly after the two were fired, a similar accident occurred and no one was discharged. Facts later brought out in court established that Elliot and Coady, in fact, bore no responsibility for the accident that led to their dismissal. Three other members of the crew were responsible for allowing the lacing steel to lie on the flanges of the street-support beams, for choking the steel beam that the crane was lifting off center, and for not attaching the tag line to the steel beam. None of them were fired. Furthermore, the procedures Elliot's crew were following when the accident occurred were specified in written instructions from superintendent Derse, and the same unsafe procedures continued in use at the work site after Coady and Elliot were fired. It was Derse who ordered lacing steel to rest on the flanges of street-support beams and to discontinue the use of tag lines—when safety inspection crews were not in the area—in order to speed up work on the project. And it was Derse who fired the two pile drivers.

In fact, the causes of the accident at Metro D-1 resulted from precisely the hazards that Elliot sought to have corrected: mechanical defects in his crew's crane and exposed 13,000-volt electrical cables. Elliot had asked project superintendent Huffman to investigate the causes of the accident and requested that he follow the company's disciplinary procedure when he was told to get off the job site. Huffman told him that P & Z could abandon its internal procedure anytime it chose to do so, especially if an employee was considered "unsafe."

As soon as Elliot was fired, he went to MIA where a representative told him "it was too bad, but there was nothing MIA could do." Elliot next went to his union headquarters, Pile Drivers Local 2311, where he was told that the union could do nothing to help him. A union official did phone P & Z on Elliot's behalf, but was told that the company was within its rights to fire men on the spot for unsafe acts. The company claimed it was only acting prudently to protect the lives of other workers who had been put in serious danger because of Elliot's and Coady's carelessness. The union did not investigate the charge. The next day, with all his other remedies exhausted, Elliot filed an 11(c) complaint with OSHA, claiming that his and Coady's firing constituted direct retaliation for their safety-and-health complaints.

OSHA treats an 11(c) complaint as a very serious matter. The act calls for a speedy investigation of such a charge and requires the Labor Department to report back to a complainant about its investigation of the charges within 90 days. OSHA investigators have the right to inspect an employer's records to establish the validity of an 11(c) charge. If the claim is proved to OSHA's satisfaction, it first attempts to negotiate a voluntary settlement with an offending employer. Failing that, OSHA can then sue the employer in federal court to restore the employee's job, lost salary, and lost benefits—plus interest.

After OSHA investigated Coady and Elliot's claim, it attempted to have the two reinstated by P & Z. But the company steadfastly refused. After more than a year of investigation and negotiation, OSHA finally filed suit against P & Z in federal court. The case came before U.S. Magistrate Henry H. Kennedy, Jr., on June 27, 1977. Elliot and Coady were represented by Rick Voigt, a Labor Department assistant counsel. At first, P & Z's claim that it had only acted prudently in firing two employees who had endangered the lives of their fellow workers through reckless action seemed a formidable defense. Through testimony, however, Voigt was able to establish that in every instance the facts were the opposite of what P & Z claimed. "Basically," says Voigt, "we took the company's explanation of what happened and made them eat it."

P & Z claimed that Elliot and Coady had endangered the lives of others. Voigt showed that seven people had been involved in the procedures that caused the accident—excluding Coady who wasn't even in the excavation when the accident occurred—and only one, Elliot, had been fired. Derse was more responsible than Elliot, Voigt showed, since he had specified the procedure that resulted in the accident. Coady's connection with the accident was shown to be unfounded. Voigt also demonstrated that Derse, the man who fired Elliot and Coady, had expressed a considerable animosity towards them prior to the accident because of their complaints about safety hazards. Despite Derse's comments that the pile drivers were lazy and just wanted to "bitch," he admitted in court that Coady and Elliot were two of the most productive pile drivers at the job site. Said Derse: "They always did the work assigned them."

Perhaps the most damaging evidence against P & Z was the undeniable fact that Elliot and Coady had complained, in writing, about the very hazards that led to the accident more than a week before it took place. To Magistrate Kennedy, it seemed more than coincidental that two men should be peremptorily fired for involvement in an accident caused by safety hazards that they had persistently sought to correct. On March 3, 1978, Magistrate Kennedy ruled in favor of the two pile drivers. He found that the accident at Metro D-1 "could not possibly serve as a proper justification for discharge." Kennedy took special note of the facts that Coady was not even at the job site and that Elliot, as foreman, was following procedures specified by his superior when the accident took place. To the company's claim that Coady's and Elliot's work was "unsafe," Kennedy replied that the two pile drivers "had never received a written reprimand for work which management may have found unsatisfactory." In Kennedy's view, P & Z's reason for firing Elliot and Coady was "a pretext."

Kennedy assessed P & Z the maximum penalty that the law allows. The company was ordered to pay Elliot $12,488 and Coady $18,458 for lost wages plus six percent interest (for the period between November 20, 1975, when they were fired, and December 7, 1976, when P & Z's contract with the Washington Metropolitan Area Transit Authority expired). The monetary judgment also included Elliot's and Coady's lost benefits, and the expense they incurred looking for new jobs.

P & Z appealed Kennedy's decision to the U.S. Circuit Court of Appeals, an action which tied up the case for another 18 months. Ultimately, the appeals court issued a summary affirmation of Kennedy's decision, calling P & Z's appeal "frivolous." In late 1979, almost four years after they were fired, Elliot and Coady received nearly $35,000 from P & Z.

"P & Z gained more than a year through their appeal," observes attorney Voigt, "and I suppose, because of double-digit inflation, that made the money less valuable to them. Even so, they received a fairly strong sanction. Thirty-five thousand dollars is still a large sum, and they had to pay some hefty legal fees. Some of the people working for P & Z at the time of the firing no longer work for them. And I think it's possible—although it's highly speculative—that they were discharged because of their conduct in the Coady and Elliot case."

The monetary judgment against P & Z, the largest ever assessed against a company in an 11(c) action, created a minor stir when it was announced. *Business Week* took note of it in an article titled "Discrimination Can Cost You." The message to employers was clear: The OSHA Act has teeth, and they can bite. In fact, the number of 11(c) complaints OSHA receives nationwide has more than quadrupled in the past six years. OSHA received 3,100 11(c) complaints in fiscal year 1979 compared to only 752 complaints in fiscal year 1974. In the coming years, the numbers may increase even more dramatically. "Lately, we have been getting a much higher number of complaints from technical people, engineers, and high-level management people who supervise production processes or operating procedures," says Rick Voigt. "I think the accident at Three Mile Island has had a tremendous impact on these kinds of people. They saw what kind of potential damage their silence on safety problems could create."

According to Voigt, 11(c) victories like the Elliot and Coady case have little to do with the increasing number of discrimination complaints. "I don't think that many employees who take the kind of action Elliot and Coady did think it out first. They know that even if OSHA steps in to help, it's going to be a fairly messy, drawn-out battle. People who are receiving discharges or discipline are now aware of their 11(c) rights. In the past they wouldn't have filed a complaint. They would have gone off and looked for another job—and been angry. Now, because of the Department of Labor's publicity campaign, union safety institutes, and OSHA compliance officers who hand out 11(c) material when they inspect a job site, these workers are aware that they have a statutory remedy available to them."

Robert Elliot is one person who knows that even when OSHA steps in, the disruption of a person's life that results from a punitive discharge can be harrowing. After he was fired, Elliot immediately began looking for another job. But, where once his skills were in much demand in the

Washington area construction industry, this time job hunting was a lot more difficult. The construction industry is a fairly closed field, Elliot says, and the contractors all know each other. Elliot quickly discovered that his reputation as a "troublemaker" had become known to almost every contractor in the area. He finally managed to find work but was laid off a short time later—a pattern that has repeated itself several times since.

Nevertheless, Elliot has few regrets about his actions at the P & Z job site. Through it all, says Elliot, he managed to maintain his self-respect by not quietly acquiescing to life-endangering practices.

# Uncovering False Reporting to the Government

## Arthur Suchodolski

From 1972 to 1976, I worked for the Michigan Consolidated Gas Company—the largest gas distribution company in Michigan—as an internal auditor. Auditing is an exacting profession that is governed by a strict code of ethics. The code demands honest appraisals of all data an auditor analyzes and the truthful reporting of facts uncovered in an audit. The Code of Ethics of the Institute of Internal Auditors states explicitly: "In his reporting, a member shall reveal such material facts known to him, which, if not revealed, could either distort the report of the results of operations under review or conceal unlawful practice."

I took my job at Michigan Consolidated seriously, especially my obligation to report any waste and inefficiency. When I uncovered evidence of mismanagement and possible fraud in the credit division of the company, however, my report was ignored by top company officials. Instead of seeking to correct the problems I had uncovered, management first reassigned me to another position and later fired me. I have challenged Michigan Consolidated in the courts in an effort to salvage my professional reputation. In the meantime, Michigan taxpayers and Michigan Consolidated consumers continue to subsidize the company's financial mismanagement.

My auditing career began in the early 1960s. I started with an accounting firm in Detroit and then moved over to a division of the General Motors Corporation in Flint, Michigan. An ambitious young auditor, I tried to improve my standing in the profession with membership in organizations such as the Institute of Internal Auditors (IIA). Through my activities in the IIA—I was elected governor of the Detroit chapter—I met Robert Thursdale, chapter president, who was general auditor for Michigan Consolidated Gas. Thursdale took a liking to me and, in June 1972, offered me a position on his staff as senior internal auditor. His offer was very attractive. In addition to a salary increase and additional fringe benefits, Thursdale offered the promise of a promotion to middle management in two or three years. I decided to accept the position and began working at Michigan Consolidated in September.

My first assignment was supervision of an operational audit of the company's purchasing and traffic, a vital area of Michigan Consolidated's day-to-day operations that gave me an excellent overview of the inner workings of the firm. An operational audit is quite different from a financial audit, which is the activity that the public most commonly associates with the auditing profession. A financial audit deals with the examination and verification of accounts within an organization; an operational audit, on the other hand, is aimed at evaluating the operations of the organization in order to help management achieve the most efficient operation possible.

In the course of my operational audit, some basic facts about Michigan Consolidated became clear to me. Internal auditors like myself were not accepted by other employees in the company. Auditors did not receive transfers to other positions of financial responsibility in the company, a situation which resulted in an unusually heavy turnover in the auditing department. I also discovered that audit reports were often dressed up to present a rosy picture to company management. These overly optimistic reports were often distortions that hid serious problems from responsible officials within the company. The heavy turnover in the auditing department at Michigan Consolidated was particularly troubling to me. Between January 1973 and August 1974, ten auditors either resigned or were fired from the company, a figure representing more than one complete turnover in the department. I had left a good job to join Michigan Consolidated and part of the attraction the company held for me was Thursdale's promise of a long-term position that offered growth potential.

However good Thursdale's intentions in making his original offer to me were, his ability to make good on it vanished in June 1973 when he resigned as general auditor. Thursdale had built up 20 years seniority at Michigan Consolidated and at other companies owned by the American Natural Resources Company—Michigan Consolidated's parent company. No one in the audit department ever found out why Thursdale forfeited his seniority by leaving suddenly. Thursdale was replaced by Gilbert Lavey, an audit manager with the certified public accounting firm of Arthur Andersen & Company, the firm that conducted the annual outside audit of Michigan Consolidated Gas. Lavey was quick to make changes in the department, firing both the operational audits manager and the financial audits manager within four months of his arrival—again without any explanation to the audit department staff. It was nearly a year before Lavey appointed a manager to replace the two he fired, and during that time members of the auditing staff reported directly to him.

The turnovers and lack of direction at Michigan Consolidated prompted me to request—in November 1974—a transfer to another job within the American Natural Resources Company organization. Michael Shea, the manager of professional employment at the company, asked me to speak to Lavey about my reasons for requesting the transfer. I met with Lavey early in December and told him why I wanted to be reassigned. Lavey told me that I was one of three people he was considering for the position of audit manager. He asked me to hold up my request for transfer until he reached a decision, which I agreed to do.

In January 1975, Lavey promoted Michael McInerney, a much less experienced man who was more than ten years younger than I, to operational audit manager. I went to see Lavey shortly after McInerney was promoted and made known my disappointment about not getting the job. Lavey said he understood my feelings and added that he had recommended me for the job of audit supervisor at the Michigan Wisconsin Pipeline Company. If that job failed to materialize, Lavey told me, he would do his best to find me a more responsible position within the American Natural Resources Organization. I accepted his word in good faith.

After three or four months passed, it became apparent to me that Lavey had no intention of following through on his promise. In addition, I had some serious doubts about McInerney's competence to supervise operational audits. When I registered objections with McInerney about audit procedures he was using that I thought were ill-advised, he told me, "Different strokes for different folks." When I tried to alert Lavey to the procedural problems in the department, he snapped, "McInerney is your manager. You report to him and not to me!" In August 1975, more than eight months after Lavey promised to help me find another job within the company, I again went to the professional employment manager and requested a transfer. As far as I know, no action was taken on my request.

Two months later, I received what was to be my last real assignment for Michigan Consolidated—an operational audit of the company's credit division. Normally, an audit of this kind requires the development of an audit program before the actual work commences. An audit program is a plan of the areas of the company's operations the auditor intends to investigate. Doing an audit without an audit plan is akin to taking a long trip without a map; you can do it, but it will probably take you much longer to get where you're going. Nevertheless, McInerney asked me to start field work on the audit without a prepared plan because he felt uncomfortable about not having any auditors in the field.

The credit division of Michigan Consolidated is responsible for approving credit for both residential and commercial users. When customers fall behind in their payments, the credit division is supposed to take action to obtain payment. During the month that I conducted my audit of the division I found that procedures there were extremely lax and that the division had a mass of problems. Work procedures were badly out of date; employees were poorly trained; internal controls on financial transactions were not in existence or were not being observed; and millions of dollars' worth of unpaid accounts from previous years were never turned over to outside collection agencies for action.

The most serious problem of mismanagement in the credit division involved the way in which tens of thousands of welfare accounts were handled. Under Michigan's Aid to Families with Dependent Children Program, welfare families receive a lump-sum payment from which they are supposed to manage their own money and pay their own rents, utility bills, and the like. Following some embarrassing publicity several years earlier over service cutoffs to welfare customers, Michigan Consolidated entered into a "sweetheart" deal with the Michigan Department of Social Services. The company agreed to inform the Department of Social Services prior to any cutoff action; in return, the state agreed to pay the bills for delinquent accounts out of the state's "emergency aid" fund.

At first, utility bill payments out of the "emergency aid" fund were modest. However, as word got out among welfare recipients, many of them decided not to pay their bills, comfortable in the knowledge that the state would cover their delinquent accounts no matter what they did. This abuse, in effect, meant that the Michigan Department of Social Services was making duplicate payments to many welfare recipients: the initial payment to the welfare family, and a second payment to Michigan Consolidated. With its incentive to collect on delinquent accounts removed by the state's guarantee of payment, Michigan Consolidated took no action to clear up arrears from welfare customers. The losers in this arrangement were the taxpayers of the state of Michigan, and Michigan Consolidated's paying customers.

Three weeks after I began my audit of the credit division, I presented the division manager with a list of more than 50 problem areas that I wanted reviewed by him or his staff before the audit was completed. At the same time, I contacted Frank Pinkelman, deputy auditor general for the state of Michigan, and told him that Michigan "sundry order forms"—the state form which Michigan Consolidated received authorizing it to bill the state for delinquent welfare customers' heating bills—were being approved by only the rubber signature stamp of the director of the Wayne County Unit of the Department of Social Services. This meant that, theoretically, anyone with access to a signature stamp could authorize payment. Pinkelman told me that an audit of the Wayne County Unit several years earlier uncovered the use of the rubber signature stamp, and that he thought the practice was ordered discontinued at the time. The state immediately began its own audit of the Wayne County Unit, which has approximately 20 offices.

On three occasions in late October, I attempted to meet with Michael McInerney to discuss the massive problems I had uncovered in the credit division. Each time he told me that he was too busy with more pressing problems to discuss the audit with me. During the same period, Gilbert Lavey made several inquiries about my progress with the credit division audit. I told Lavey that the audit was being conducted without the benefit of an audit program—at McInerney's direction—but that I did not feel too uncomfortable working without a program, since this was only the initial audit of the division. At the end of October, my assistant on the credit division audit was assigned to another task by McInerney, and I was left to perform the audit alone.

On October 31, 1975, I sent a five-page memo to Michael McInerney (with a copy to Lavey) outlining my preliminary findings in the credit division audit and explaining why I thought additional time was necessary to complete the job adequately. A week later, McInerney told me that he was relieving me of responsibility for the audit, saying that he would prepare the final audit report on the credit division himself. When I left the credit division audit, it was approximately two-thirds completed. To the best of my knowledge, the job was never finished by McInerney or anyone else.

McInerney transferred me to a "non-audit special assignment" in the company's information systems department—a project in which the company's personnel records were programmed into a computer. I had absolutely no background in computers and had never been a computer auditor, so the field was completely new to me. It was evident from the start that the assignment was a do-nothing-and-wait situation.

On the morning of November 17, Michael McInerney called me into his office and showed me a written "performance appraisal" of my work that he had prepared. He characterized my overall job perform- ance as "poor," noting among other things that I did not "develop [audit] plans, and [that I audited] on a hit-or-miss basis." The reference, I assumed, was to my work on the credit division audit, undertaken without a plan at McInerney's express order. The manager and I ex- changed harsh words over this and I stormed out of his office.

I immediately went to Gilbert Lavey's office and asked for an op- portunity to speak to him at his earliest convenience. Two weeks passed with no response from Lavey. I finally managed to approach him in a hallway one day, and tried to discuss McInerney's written evaluation of my work. Lavey cut me short, telling me that if I was dissatisfied with my position I was free to look for work elsewhere in the company. Of course, Lavey knew that I had been doing just that for nearly a year and that he himself had promised to help me.

On January 16, 1976, Michael McInerney called me into his office and requested that I review a draft of the credit division audit report that he had prepared. He told me that he needed my comments within three days. I examined the report, which listed me as auditor-in-charge, very carefully. On Monday, January 19, I gave McInerney an eight-page memo listing the items that I felt needed revision or clarification in the document. I also told McInerney that I could not sign the report as auditor-in-charge unless all the audit findings were included, along with an explanation as to the areas of the credit division operation that were not examined. McInerney said he would think it over.

Ten days later, on January 29, Gilbert Lavey called me into his office and told me I was being fired, effective the following day. He added that I would be paid administrative leave for another month. I asked Lavey his reasons for firing me. He replied, "You disturb the operations of this office." That afternoon I broke the bad news to my wife and four sons, who range in age from six to 16. It was a hard blow for all of us. Even so, I had a great deal of confidence in my abilities as an auditor, and I was certain that finding a new job would be a simple matter. But as things turned out, I couldn't have been more wrong about my job prospects.

About a year-and-a-half before Lavey fired me, I had attended a joint meeting of the audit staffs of Michigan Consolidated and the Michigan Wisconsin Pipeline Company. The purpose of the meeting was to discuss the role of auditing in the two companies and the role of the audit committee of the board of directors of American Natural Resources, the parent company of both firms. R. J. Blank, the general auditor for American Natural, stressed to us the importance of independent auditors in the American Natural system. "Auditors," Blank told us, "have free and confidential access to any committee member on any significant item involving management control after efforts to have their superiors report such items have failed." After I was fired, I took Blank's message to heart and attempted to alert top management to the serious problems in Michigan Consolidated's credit division.

On February 6, I wrote a letter to Arthur Seder, Jr., president of American Natural Resources. "As a certified internal auditor," I wrote, "I have an obligation to my profession and to my employer to abide by the code of ethics. . . . In regard to a recent audit and other matters, I request an opportunity to appear before the audit committee of the board of directors. My appearance will be in the best interests of management and customers of Michigan Consolidated Gas Company."

As a result of my letter, a meeting was arranged between myself and Paul Jasperse, the partner from Arthur Andersen and Company— Gilbert Lavey's old firm—who supervised the annual outside audit of Michigan Consolidated. I gave Jasperse a chronological account of my experiences with Michigan Consolidated from the time I began the credit division audit until the day I was fired. I also told him about the many problems in the company's audit department, especially the inordinately large turnover which resulted in a lack of adequately trained professional staff. Jasperse asked me specific questions about the credit division audit. Later, we were joined by Russell Whitfield, who had succeeded R. J. Blank as general auditor of American Natural Resources. He, too, asked me many questions about the credit division audit.

A few weeks later, on March 4, I received a letter from Arthur Seder. He told me that both Jasperse and Whitfield reported to him on the meeting we had, and that the matter was discussed with the chairman of the audit committee of American Natural Resources, Robert Semple. "However, in view of the thorough review we have made of the areas of concern," Seder informed me, "we have concluded that nothing further would be gained by your personal appearance before the American Natural audit committee."

I was taken aback by Seder's high-handed dismissal of the serious mismanagement I had brought to his attention. The only conclusion I could draw from his action was that the company's stated policy of making the audit committee available to auditors was mere window dressing for the Michigan Public Service Commission, the watchdog agency that traditionally puts great stock in the work of certified independent auditors like myself. A month after I received Seder's letter, I made one final attempt to resolve the matter amicably. I wrote a letter to Semple, requesting a meeting with his audit committee. He phoned me at home several days later, but hung up angrily when I refused to discuss the problem with him over the telephone.

Early in March, I retained V. Paul Donnelly, a Detroit attorney specializing in employee dissent cases, to represent me in my dispute with Michigan Consolidated. Donnelly advised me to file an age-discrimination complaint with both the U.S. Department of Labor and the Michigan Department of Civil Rights on the grounds that I had been passed over for the operational audit manager's job at the company in favor of McInerney, and that that action had resulted in my being forced out of my job. I was 42 when McInerney was promoted, while he was barely 30. By the end of March, I had filed both complaints.

On May 7, the Labor Department informed me that it was unable to settle my dispute with Michigan Consolidated. Under the law, the Labor Department has 60 days from the time a complaint is filed to investigate the problem. If they find that the complaint has merit, all the department can do is attempt to reconcile the dispute; the department does not have the power to reconcile the dispute itself or to take any legal action. However, a Labor Department representative did confirm that I had met the necessary requirements for an age-discrimination case. He advised me that I could bring a civil suit against Michigan Consolidated if I wished to do so.

Meanwhile, after four fruitless months of job-hunting, I went through a period of severe depression. My wife's worries about our family's future resulted in substantial weight loss, and my sons were disturbed about the limited amount of time I could spend with them. I dearly wanted to pay more attention to my wife and children but nearly all of my time was taken by my search for another job.

Just when things seemed hopeless, I received a phone call from a former colleague who told me about a temporary job with an accounting project involving the family holdings of the chairman of the Detroit and Mackinac Railroad. The job was in Tawas City, about 170 miles north of my home in the Detroit area. To my surprise, I got the job, and commuted to Tawas City for the next six months. I would drive north early every Monday morning, returning home the following Friday night to spend the weekends with my family. In Tawas City, I lived in a camper-trailer loaned to me by my brother-in-law. The money I saved by living this way enabled me to pay some of my debts.

The lonely evenings in Tawas City gave me precious time to analyze my experiences at Michigan Consolidated. I knew I lost my job because I spoke out about company mismanagement, but it was my duty as an auditor to do so. I decided to write letters about what had happened to me to state officials and others I knew in the auditing profession. If management at Michigan Consolidated wouldn't listen to me and the Labor Department couldn't help me, at least I could make the facts known about Michigan Consolidated's breach of its public trust in the way in which it dealt with welfare customers' arrears.

To my surprise, many of my letters were answered. As a result, I met with officials of the Michigan Public Service Commission. In addition, I again wrote letters to officials at Michigan Consolidated in an attempt to get them to give me their attention. Michigan Consolidated's executive vice president, R. W. Stewart, rejected my request. In his reply, he wrote: "I hope that you can proceed to develop your and your family's future and put your mind to this purpose and effort, rather than continue to attempt to reopen a matter that is closed." I refused to give in so easily and wrote back: "Only the Lord knows the reasons why I refuse to accept the answer that this matter is closed. In order to clear my name and reputation, I will continue to pursue this matter—through the courts, if necessary."

In November 1976, the results of the internal audit of the Wayne County Unit of the Michigan Department of Social Services—originally prompted by my phone call to Frank Pinkelman a year before—was made public, and received extensive coverage by the local media. Preliminary investigations revealed that more than $1 million may have been lost through theft, fraud, and sloppy management in the Wayne County unit. The audit report—which noted the existence of "an environment in which fraud may flourish"—uncovered widespread over-payments to suppliers for services provided to welfare recipients. Significantly, the report did not mention the problem of duplicate heating payments to welfare recipients.

On December 2, 1976, I wrote a letter to the director of the Michigan Department of Social Services about the problem of duplicate heating payments by the Wayne County unit, and a meeting was arranged with the director of his internal audit division in which I gave him the details of my audit of the credit division at Michigan Consolidated. Less than one year after this meeting, a headline in the *Detroit Free Press* announced: "State Cheated Out of $19 Million in Heating Aid to the Poor." The article went on to detail the abuses I had uncovered almost two years earlier. Earlier, on January 13, 1977, the *Detroit News* reported that Michigan Consolidated was unable to collect $6 million in gas bills for the year 1976—and the deficit would have to be made up by customers who do pay their bills.

A few days after the *Detroit News* story appeared, I again wrote to Arthur Seder and Robert Semple about the problem of uncollectible accounts. On February 15, Semple wrote back saying, "This is really a matter that falls within the domain of management, and until such time as management or our outside auditor, Arthur Andersen and Company, approaches the audit committee for consideration, we would not wish to consider it." I found Semple's reply particularly upsetting. It convinced me that the audit committee acted solely in response to the wishes of management, and failed to take into account the interest of the company's customers and shareholders.

On April 25, 1977, the Michigan Department of Civil Rights informed me that their investigation into my age-discrimination complaint against Michigan Consolidated did not disclose evidence to support my claim. They concluded that my firing was the result of "poor work performance." The company had provided the civil rights department investigator with copies of written work appraisals, all done after Michael McInerney was appointed manager, and all showing a decline in my job performance. Michigan Consolidated claimed that I had been a "troublemaker" from the very first day I started work there, that I had difficulty focusing on the company's operational methods, and that I was unable to take direction or constructive criticism. My effectiveness as an auditor was limited, the company maintained, because I was "always looking for crooks and some kind of skullduggery."

Most of these claims about my job performance were made by a Michigan Consolidated attorney I had never met, but who, nevertheless, considered himself knowledgeable about my auditing abilities and personal character. When I attempted to have the decision reconsidered by the civil rights department's review board, my appeal was denied because of what the board considered a lack of "specific grounds." The civil rights department did inform me that "an appeal may be filed with the appropriate circuit court in the State of Michigan—if you wish to pursue the matter."

I was very disappointed by the findings of the Michigan Civil Rights Department, but I felt there were still avenues open to me to clear my name short of civil suit. Shortly after I received the civil rights department's findings, I learned that the Michigan attorney general's office was investigating Michigan Consolidated's request for a $110 million rate increase, an amount which far exceeded President Carter's wage and price guidelines. I wrote to the attorney general and several months later, under oath, I testified about the arrears situation at Michigan Consolidated and about how the huge sum that the company made no effort to collect was partially responsible for the enormous rate increase request. In September 1978, the Michigan Public Service Commission rejected Michigan Consolidated's request, and allowed the company to raise its rates by only $19.7 million. Naturally, I was quite gratified by the findings of the commission. But I was not finished yet; I still felt strongly about the need to clear my name and restore my reputation.

In August 1978, my attorney filed suit in Wayne County Circuit Court against Michigan Consolidated. The suit charged that the utility had breached its employment agreement with me by failing to evaluate my job performance objectively; that the company's act of firing me with only 24-hours' notice "maliciously and in bad faith" decreased my right to employment; that my firing constituted age discrimination; that my firing because of complaints about mismanagement constituted a retaliatory discharge; and that because Michigan Consolidated is a public utility, my firing constituted unlawful state action.

Early in 1979, the circuit judge dismissed my suit on the grounds that I had no basis on which to sue. The judge said that an employer can terminate an employer-employee relationship at any time for any reason, barring statutory protections or written agreements to the contrary. My attorney is appealing my case, which is scheduled to be heard before the Michigan Court of Appeals early in 1980.

The last four years have been hard on my family and me. My career as an internal auditor was effectively destroyed—for the past three years I have been working as the controller of a shoe-retailing company in the Detroit area. Through it all, however, I have not lost faith in my abilities. And my principles have stood the test. My fight for vindication in the courts will take time, but I have faith that it will result in a victory for me and other individuals of conscience in the corporate world.

In the meantime, I feel as if I have been at least partially vindicated. On March 8, 1979, I again testified before the Michigan Public Service Commission on behalf of the ratepayer who is being asked to pick up the costs of Michigan Consolidated's uncollectibles. These figures have risen from $2.6 million in 1974 to $12.3 million in 1978—the later figure representing 70 percent of the company's total earnings of $17.4 million for the year 1978. It seems to me that these figures demonstrate the company's mismanagement more dramatically than anything I could ever do or say. The Michigan attorney general in his report, taking exception to Michigan Consolidated's rate request for the additional $102 million, stated:

> Michigan Consolidated wants an uncollectibles allowance of approximately $15 million, an amount which would represent a 100% increase over the allowance for uncollectibles provided for [currently]. . . . We have the benefit of substantial unrebutted testimony from former internal auditor Arthur Suchodolski giving us vivid details of how the company bungled its collectibles and was subject to internal criticism from auditors on numerous occasions. In short, despite Michigan Consolidated's protests to the contrary, the competent, material and substantial evidence on the record indicates that Michigan Consolidated does not do as good a job on its uncollectibles as other similar utilities and that there is substantial evidence to support the conclusion that responsibility lies within the company. . . .

# Refusing to Drive Unsafe Vehicles

## Leo Kohls

I had been working as a driver for United Parcel
Service (UPS) for eight years when my refusal to
take out unsafe vehicles led to a campaign of
harassment by company officials that finally resulted
in my being fired, in 1975, for "insubordination."
Although I have been unable to find steady work
since I was discharged by UPS—and despite the fact
that a long, drawn out legal suit between UPS and
me is still going on—I do not regret having insisted
that UPS live up to federal safety regulations and its
own rules.

As a driver of tractor-trailer trucks, I quickly
became aware of the serious hazards involved in my
work. The job requires long hours on the road, and
during my eight years of interstate runs I saw many
accidents and near accidents. It didn't take me long
to realize how important it is for a driver to be at
his best and to have safe equipment to operate.
Because truck drivers have to share the highways
with the general public, I felt a concern not only for
my own safety but also for the safety of other
motorists whose lives might be jeopardized if I took
out a defective rig. If you look at the statistics for

road accidents involving tractor-trailer trucks, you will understand my road fears.

According to the most recently published figures by the United States Department of Transportation, of the 50,000 highway fatalities in 1978, heavy trucks were responsible for 5,075 deaths, despite the fact that they account for less than one percent of the vehicles on the road. The number of truck fatalities was up 53 percent over 1975. During the same period, all vehicle fatalities were up only 12 percent, and this increase was due primarily to the increase in truck fatalities. There is no doubt that heavy trucks are dangerous, or that they are becoming increasingly so.

Up until my last two years with UPS, I never had any problems with my employers. My work record, in fact, was a very good one. I should mention that I am not a native-born American. I was born in Poland and came to this country in 1952, when I was 15. I went to high school here and, after getting my diploma in 1955, I joined the U.S. Marine Corps. I was honorably discharged in 1958 with the rank of corporal. After my discharge from the Marines, I went to work in the retail field. I worked for S.S. Kresge and was, for a while, the assistant manager in several of their Cleveland, Ohio, stores. Because working in the retail field involved frequent relocation, I decided to look for a job that would allow me to settle in one place so I could raise a family.

In October 1967, I went to work for United Parcel Service (UPS) in Columbus, Ohio, as a truck driver. UPS originally trained me for a city driving position. Later, in 1969, I was given additional training for a road driving position in tractor-trailers. At the time UPS was expanding its operations to include cross-country delivery service. The company was really putting a lot of effort into its training program for drivers in order to make a favorable impression on the Interstate Commerce Commission (ICC) and the Department of Transportation (DOT), which were considering UPS's application for cross-country certification.

I made a point of participating in all of the company's special training programs, often on my own time. During the company's expansion period, UPS's aim was to have the safest equipment and the best-trained drivers on the road, and in my opinion we did. We were the elite among cross-country truck drivers—the best. In its manual of safety regulations, UPS digests DOT regulations and emphasizes the driver's obligation to obey them. Under the heading "Don't Drive Unsafe Vehicle," the following DOT regulation is quoted: "No vehicle should be put in service until any defect, likely to cause an accident or breakdown of the vehicle, has been corrected."

After UPS obtained the government authorizations it wanted, drivers found it more difficult to get repairs on their equipment. The company's special training programs were discontinued. The basic training remained for the new drivers, but it was a token program used to satisfy DOT regulations and to provide the company with a way of shifting the blame to the driver in the event of an accident. If a driver discovered a problem with the equipment, he usually had to make a fuss with management to get the repairs. Most of the time, the driver lost on the issue and was ordered out on the road with the defective equipment. Supervisors often told us not to worry about being stopped by the police, that since we kept our trucks bright and shiny they wouldn't bother us. Eventually most of the drivers got so discouraged that they would take out any rig just so they would not be subject to harassment from management.

The situation got worse for me in 1973 because I continued to insist that necessary repairs be made on trucks I drove—not only for my own safety but for the benefit of everyone who used the highways. In October 1974 I was told by Paul Chambers, a UPS supervisor, that my personnel file had been turned over to an attorney, which was his way of telling me that UPS would get rid of me if I did not do as I was told and stop complaining about the equipment. I was instructed to sign vehicle inspection reports without checking the equipment. In the past, the mechanics signed the reports after inspecting the equipment. By signing the report, the mechanic was certifying that the equipment was safe for the highways. According to the government regulations, drivers are not permitted—because they're really not qualified—to certify a vehicle to be mechanically safe. I notified the ICC about the problem and was told by the Columbus, Ohio, office to take this matter to the DOT and the Teamsters Union.

At about this time, two of my supervisors, Robert Fornof, division manager, and Henry Sherman, feeder manager, began calling me into their offices on a daily basis to discuss my performance. They constantly complained that I took too long to perform my job, that I spent too much time at the automotive shop for what they claimed were unnecessary repairs, that I exceeded my lunch and break time, and that I took too long driving to my destination. One day Fornof would tell me to stop at a certain place for my break; the next day Sherman would change that location for one he preferred. Then Fornof would criticize me because I had not stopped where he had ordered me to stop. The two managers played this game for some time so they could build a record against me for insubordination and failure to follow instructions.

In January of 1975, UPS manager Bob McCain called the local Teamsters Union office and requested a formal hearing on charges being brought against me by the company. I knew I wouldn't get much help from Teamsters Local 413, the one I belonged to, because I had frequently objected to corrupt practices by the union leadership. (Shortly after I was fired in 1975, Local president Vito Mango and business agent James Kirk were indicted, tried, and convicted in a federal court. Mango received a six-year sentence for a "pattern of racketeering activity" that included embezzlement of union funds; Kirk was sentenced to 15 months for having lied to the grand jury that investigated Mango.) At the hearing, the company charged me with failure to follow instructions and poor job performance. I was suspended for two weeks without pay.

At this point, I realized that the campaign to have me fired was in earnest. I appealed the suspension to the joint union management grievance committee, but I knew that the best I could hope for was a deadlock. The Teamsters Union, unlike most unions, has no grievance procedure that provides for final settlement by an impartial arbitrator. Instead, there are joint labor-management grievance committees consisting of an equal number of union and management officials, with no impartial representative who can cast a tie-breaking vote. Company officials are supposed to be chosen from districts other than the one where the grievance is being held. But in point of fact, all company managers, wherever they are based, have the same attitude towards drivers who "talk back" and complain about unsafe trucks. For these reasons, Teamsters generally regard the grievance committees as "kangaroo courts."

As might be expected, my suspension was upheld by the grievance panel. I returned to work and the conditions I had complained about continued. Two months later, the company requested another hearing with the local union. This time I was charged with failing to follow instructions regarding the use of work hours, abusing company equipment, and continually complaining about the condition of the equipment that I had to operate.

At this hearing UPS informed the union that I was being fired. I appealed my discharge to the joint grievance committee, and the dismissal was later reduced to a three-week suspension without pay. During this second grievance committee hearing, I asked permission to present some witnesses and requested the committee to check Article 17 of our union contract with UPS. Article 17 states: "The Employer shall not require employees to take out on the streets or highways any vehicle that is not in safe operating condition or equipped with the safety appliances prescribed by law." I was then asked by a company representative if I was threatening the panel. From what I knew about our union leadership, I realized that Vito Mango, the local's president, and business agent James Kirk were merely going through the formality of presenting my case to this kangaroo court. But I had to go through with this process to establish my case.

Shortly afterward, I wrote to the Secretary of Labor's office in Washington, D.C. That office suggested that I contact the National Labor Relations Board (NLRB) in Cincinnati, Ohio, where I filed charges against UPS. I also wrote to the DOT in Washington, D.C., and to its regional office in Illinois. I prepared a list of equipment defects and I turned it over to the DOT. A DOT investigator was sent from the regional office to check out my complaint. While the investigator was at the Columbus UPS terminal, a stack of equipment defect write-ups mysteriously disappeared. Some were found stashed in the men's restroom. The DOT investigator told me that it was a violation for UPS merely to ask a driver to pull a defective truck when the defect violated state, local, or federal laws. He asked me to keep the DOT informed of the situation because he had talked to company officials and they had assured him that things were going to be changed. Finally, the investigator suggested that I keep a record of future problems and stated that if he had to come back, serious measures would be taken.

In the weeks that followed, I continued to have difficulties in getting proper repairs. So I began to take out the defective vehicles with the intention of having them cited by the highway patrol for safety violations. Once out on the highways I would look for a State Trooper and then ask to have the truck inspected. Even though I had to take time off to go to court to answer the citations, it seemed to be the only way to try and improve the situation. Although UPS had to pay the fine, I once had to travel hundreds of miles to appear in court. In addition, I asked other drivers to check the trucks for defects and then had them give me a signed note stating what they found wrong with the equipment. The defects included brakes that did not hold properly, oil-soaked brake linings, broken brake drums, worn tires, bad wheel seals, and problems with headlights.

Each time I had a truck cited for violations, company officials got angry and tried to put the squeeze on me to stop. Every time I was ordered to pull a defective truck I would also file a grievance—with a copy for the company, a copy for the union, and one copy for the DOT. In June 1975 UPS held another hearing to discuss my grievances. At this meeting, Jim Kirk, the union business manager, told UPS manager Bob

Fornof that he would withdraw my grievances. Both Kirk and Fornof became very angry with me because I would not go along with them.

In July, shortly after I had another truck cited for violations, I was again summoned to a hearing by Fornof. He warned me then not to stop Highway Patrol officers and ask them to inspect the equipment. In September, Fornof and Kirk again called me to a hearing, threatening me with dismissal if I did not stop filing grievances.

Again I contacted the DOT office in Homewood, Illinois, sending them a copy of each grievance I had filed along with copies of police citations against the trucks I drove. Mr. Wesley Bridwell, director of the Office of Motor Carrier Safety, assigned the case to Mr. Carl Wolfinger, the local agent from the Columbus, Ohio, office. Meanwhile, the NLRB refused to issue a complaint against the company on the charge I filed after my first dismissal in March. On August 1, 1975, Thomas M. Sheeran, the acting regional director in Cincinnati, wrote to the Columbus attorney I had engaged and informed him: "The investigation disclosed that Mr. Kohls was suspended and then discharged for his abuse of company property and for refusing to follow company instructions regarding the use of his work hours. While Kohls continuously complained about the condition of the company's equipment, there was insufficient evidence to establish that his discharge was for refusal to operate equipment which did not comply with relevant statutes or regulations or that his discharge was in reprisal for any union or protected concerted activity."

I appealed this decision to the NLRB office of appeals in Washington, D.C. The appeal was also denied. Later I discovered that the investigating officer sent out by the NLRB had not spoken to the people whose names I had given him. During a subsequent trip to Washington, I visited the NLRB office and there was told that it did not matter whether or not the investigating officer had talked with any of those people because the NLRB operated under the *Spielberg* ruling. This was an NLRB decision that established the policy of dismissing complaints where the issues had been resolved by a union-management grievance procedure provided by contract—in my case, the joint labor-management grievance committee hearing.

Up to this point I felt I had done everything that I could. My local attorney told me he could no longer advise me because of my status with the Teamsters Union and the fact that he was representing other unions in Columbus, Ohio. Finding a good local attorney was impossible, particularly in a situation that involved a large company, a powerful union, and government agencies. Then I contacted the Professional

Drivers Council for Safety and Health (PROD). I joined this organization in September 1975 and started to get advice about my rights. Later I joined two other dissident truck driver groups: Teamsters for a Decent Contract (TDC) and "UPSurge," a UPS employees group. This led to even greater hostility towards me by the Teamsters Union and UPS. The union and UPS referred to the dissidents as communists, claiming that our goal was to destroy the company, the Teamsters Union, and this country. (Bob Fornof referred to me as the Red Baron.) UPS manager Henry Sherman would later testify (at my NLRB trial in 1977) that I had said my goal was "to bring UPS and this country to its knees." In fact, I never made such a ridiculous statement to him or anyone else.

After the NLRB dismissed my first set of charges, UPS felt that they had an open door to get rid of me. The Board's decision was handed won in October 1975. I was away on vacation from October 10 to November 5. When I returned to work, I was continually followed and harassed by UPS management.

On November 12, 1975, matters came to a head. Another driver, Ed Ater, brought in a loaded tractor trailer with bad brakes. When I started my shift, he told me to carefully check the brakes on that truck, which had been assigned to me for a run to Lexington, Kentucky, because they were not holding properly. During my pretrip inspection, I found that the brakes on that trailer were still defective. I drove the truck around to the shop for repairs. After several hours of work by two mechanics I tested the truck again and found that the front trailer axle still had no braking power at all. Finally, a third mechanic was called to the scene. After inspecting and test driving the vehicle, this mechanic, James East, decided that this trailer would need new brake linings (or shoes).

In a letter he later wrote at my request, East stated: "I drove the rig and found that there were no brakes on the front axle. I tried pouring sand in the drum and also pouring brake cleaning solvent on the shoes, but still no brakes. To my knowledge, the only way to lock up the front wheels was to install new shoes."

East went to George Hurt, the repair shop supervisor, and told him that new brake linings were needed and it would take about an hour to get them. Hurt cancelled the order. He told East not to bother about the new linings, saying that the brakes were probably hot and that if the truck were allowed to sit and cool off it would "probably be all right." Hurt later claimed that he fully tested the truck, but that would have been impossible because I was in the shop with the vehicle the entire time except for a brief period when I went to a restroom.

Hurt then told my supervisor, Henry Sherman, that the rig "was ready to go." I was called to Hurt's office along with union shop steward Bob Marshall and was told by Hurt that the brakes had been tested and that they were functioning properly. I was then ordered by Sherman to pull the rig and to get started on my run to Lexington, Kentucky. I refused to pull the unit that three mechanics had concluded needed new brake linings. Sherman then told me: "Leo, by failing to follow my instructions you are placing your job on the line." We argued for a while and finally I was sent to lunch and then to the car wash to finish out the day.

I subsequently learned that another driver was put on the Lexington, Kentucky, run with the truck I refused to take out. He was informed by a UPS supervisor that there was nothing wrong with this particular trailer. In fact, however, this driver had a serious problem in Cincinnati, Ohio, and almost got involved in an accident when attempting to slow down quickly after a car pulled in front of him.

Two weeks later, on November 26, 1975, a final union–company hearing was held and at that meeting I was fired. During the first part of the hearing, James Kirk loudly criticized me for my involvement with PROD, TDC, UPSurge, and also for my stand against the local's handling of union funds. After the union representative finished chewing me out, UPS took over. The company officials ticked off the charges—including insubordination and poor job performance—and then told me that I was fired.

Immediately after my discharge I sought and obtained legal assistance from PROD attorney Arthur Fox. (I had read about similar cases involving truck drivers and knew that Mr. Fox was instrumental in helping those drivers win their cases.) On December 3, 1975, I filed charges with the NLRB against UPS and the Teamsters Union. This time, the NLRB issued a complaint against UPS, but not against the union. I was told by the NLRB attorney that he had instructions from his superiors not to bring the union into this case.

At this first hearing, administrative law judge Ralph Winkler dismissed the complaint and ordered me to go through the union-company grievance procedure. But this time I decided not to file another futile grievance because of the hostility between the union and me. I knew only too well that I would not get a fair and just hearing at another joint grievance committee hearing. Mr. Fox appealed Judge Winkler's ruling to the full Board. In March 1977 the NLRB in Washington, D.C., revised Judge Winkler's decision and sent my case back to be heard on its merits.

The NLRB trial finally took place in the summer of 1977. Prior to the trial UPS tried to have the case moved to Miami, Florida, so it would not cause any hardship for two of their witnesses—knowing full well that I would not have been financially able to bear the travel cost for myself or any of my witnesses. During the trial, UPS brought in an expert witness, an engineer from the Raybestos company which manufactures brake linings. Mr. Fox, a former NLRB lawyer, explained that it was rare for experts to testify about such technical subjects at NLRB trials. Fortunately, he knew Paul Norris, a PROD member from North Carolina who had previously worked as a mechanic for Ford production car drivers, including A. J. Foyt and Mario Andretti, and he persuaded Mr. Norris to testify on my behalf. It was like finding a needle in a haystack. Mr. Norris was more highly qualified than the UPS expert and he provided the necessary technical credibility that UPS probably figured we would never be able to establish.

UPS also produced another surprise witness named Rusty Hays to testify that in October 1975 I asked him, on many occasions, to replace perfectly good tires on my vehicles in the vicinity of Pittsburgh, Pennsylvania. In fact, not only was I on vacation that month, but my regularly assigned run took me south of Columbus to Lexington, Kentucky, not east to Pittsburgh. During Hays's testimony it was revealed that manager Henry Sherman had actually written a letter making this claim —and then had Hays sign it. By means of a subpoena, I requested my personnel file, payroll records, and other documents from UPS to prove that I was not even working during that time—that, in fact, I was on vacation during that period. UPS refused to honor that subpoena. At an earlier unemployment hearing, UPS appealed a referee's decision to grant me unemployment benefits on the grounds that the referee refused to allow the company to introduce that file—a good example of trying to have things both ways. UPS had used the unemployment insurance hearing as a "fishing trip" to see what I might use in my defense at the NLRB hearing.

Judge Winkler's decision was finally issued on September 18, 1978. Judge Winkler stated: "In refusing to pull what he claimed to be an unsafe trailer, Kohls was asserting a right under Article XVII of the operative [union-management] agreement. The assertion of such right is protected concerted activity under the [National Labor Relations] Act if his claimed belief was honestly held, regardless of its correctness." He also concluded that my refusal to drive what I reasonably believed to have been an abnormally dangerous vehicle fell within the protection of another little-known provision of the act which Mr. Fox discussed in my brief.

The Judge ordered UPS to rehire me and to give me full back pay. The company was also ordered to post a notice to employees stating:

"WE WILL NOT discharge or take any other reprisal against employees for asserting rights under collective-bargaining agreements.

"WE WILL NOT in any other manner interfere with, restrain, or coerce our employees in exercising their rights under the National Labor Relations Act."

UPS appealed this decision to the full NLRB, and six months later the Board upheld the administrative law judge's decision. It had taken three years and four months just to get this case through the NLRB. In our brief to the full Board, we asked for attorneys' fees, which the Board denied.

Promptly after the Board's decision was received, UPS filed an appeal in the federal appeals court in Cincinnati. However, Mr. Fox had filed a similar appeal on the attorneys' fees question a day earlier with the appeals court in the District of Columbia. In an attempt to get the case transferred to Cincinnati, where UPS probably figured it might have a better chance of overturning a government agency decision, UPS's lawyers claimed that they were prejudiced because they had not received the Board's decision until the day they filed their appeal. However, Mr. Fox went to the NLRB's offices in Washington and located the registered mail return receipt showing that UPS's lawyers had actually received the decision on the day before, when we had filed our appeal. In August 1979 it was decided that the appeal would be heard in Washington. Once again, we had fortunately managed to foil UPS in its relentless string of legal maneuvers to punish an employee who stood up for his rights.

Since my discharge in 1975, I have not been able to obtain steady employment as a driver or for that matter, anything else. UPS has managed to "blackball" me by refusing to release information about my driving record, a prerequisite to obtaining employment as a driver with other interstate motor carriers. Some companies have turned me down because, as a result of my filing NLRB charges against UPS, they consider me a troublemaker. Other firms give me no reasons during the interview, but later when I call back about job possibilities, they claim that they have lost my application. (I have had this said to me more than once.) Other companies don't bother to give any reason at all.

Even the local school board in Ohio where I have had some part-time work as a school bus driver refused to hire me full-time. The reasons given me were that I was new in the community, that I was too assertive, and that I would cause trouble by reporting them for any safety violations I found. This is in spite of the fact that my supervisor was pleased with my work and driving ability.

Sometime after my dismissal from UPS, I contacted Mr. Bridwell of the Illinois DOT regional office about my being fired for refusing to operate unsafe equipment. He told me in an offhand way to "work out a deal" with the company—if and when I got back to work. DOT field agent Wolfinger jokingly compared his salary with that of a truck driver and said, "You guys are well paid to take risks."

I would like to emphasize that the attitude of the DOT people not only affects the drivers but all who use the highways. Their rules about safety may look good on paper, but they are meaningless unless enforced. Many of the Department of Transportation people I met seemed indifferent about enforcing the rules and protecting the motoring public. I remember once being told by a government official that UPS always keeps its trucks washed and shiny—the point being that a truck that looks good must be in good condition. I asked this fellow what would be the difference if he got hit by a clean or a dirty truck without brakes. He became annoyed and told me to take my problem to the union or the NLRB.

Federal law and Department of Transportation regulations do not provide a worker in the trucking industry with effective and quick remedies for refusing to work in an unsafe environment. Happily, this situation may be changing. As a result of a petition from PROD, the Federal Motor Carrier Safety Regulations regarding inspection, repair, and maintenance were recently strengthened; but the changes have twice been delayed and have yet to be implemented.

The new rules call for the following procedures. First, a driver is required to inspect his vehicle before and after each day's work. If he reports a safety defect, the carrier "shall effect repair of any items listed on the vehicle inspection report(s)." The mechanic who makes the repairs must sign his name to the vehicle inspection report certifying that the repair has been made. The DOT hopes that this will encourage greater care by holding an individual liable for any failure to make a repair. A copy of the vehicle report must remain in the vehicle so that the next driver can check it to see that any necessary repairs have been made.

Furthermore, if a vehicle "by reason of its mechanical condition or loading would likely cause an accident or breakdown" it must be marked "out of service." The revised regulations then state: "No motor carrier shall require or permit any person to operate nor shall any person operate any motor vehicle declared or marked 'out of service' until all repairs required by the 'out of service notice' have been satisfactorily completed."

In addition, legislation that would protect drivers from employer reprisals for complying with the law—which PROD has been backing for nearly a decade—has finally received hearings in the U.S. Senate, where it has also been approved by a committee and referred for a final vote. However, the House of Representatives has not yet acted to close this loophole in the law. Until Congress acts, drivers will continue to live in a constant state of fear that they will be fired for complying with safety laws that may not only save their own lives but the lives of countless other motorists as well.

If these improvements in the law are strictly enforced—and that's a big if—then maybe we'll see a real improvement in the conditions under which drivers have to work. But even in the best of circumstances, the driver is still at the mercy of his employers, union bosses (if he's in a union), and government agencies—if they refuse to help for whatever reason. In the end, the court may be his only hope—that is, if he can afford to take legal action and can find an attorney who is willing to help. I was fortunate in finding a good lawyer, but the case has dragged on for over four years and I am still without a full-time job. So you have to be prepared to pay a heavy price when you stand up for your rights.

# Asserting Professional Ethics against Dangerous Drug Tests

## Dr. Grace Pierce*

In the spring of 1971, Dr. A. Grace Pierce joined the
research staff of Ortho Pharmaceutical Corporation
as associate director of medical research. A specialist
in obstetrics and gynecology, Dr. Pierce brought to
her new job an impressive set of credentials that
included 11 years as a private medical practitioner,
service in the Bureau of Medicine of the Food and
Drug Administration, and four years as a researcher
with Hoffman-La Roche, Inc. Dr. Pierce also brought
with her a professional quality that was not listed
on her résumé: a firm commitment to medical ethics
and a belief in the inviolability of the Hippocratic
Oath.

It was this strong sense of ethics that resulted in
her coming into conflict with her corporate
superiors. Ordered to proceed with tests on humans
of a new drug containing what she and her fellow
researchers considered an excessively high level of

*Written by Henry I. Kurtz

saccharin—a chemical sweetener some scientists believe may cause cancer—she refused. As Dr. Pierce later stated:* "I couldn't in good conscience take the high saccharin formulation out and give it to infants and old people when I knew there was a controversy over whether this could or could not be carcinogenic."

As a result of her stand, Dr. Pierce was stripped of her research projects, demoted in rank, and told by her immediate supervisor that corporate management considered her irresponsible and unpromotable. Faced with what she viewed as an untenable and humiliating situation, Dr. Pierce submitted her resignation, on June 17, 1975, and took her fight to uphold professional ethics into the courts.

Standing up for her beliefs was not a new experience for Dr. Pierce. Ten years earlier she resigned her post as a medical officer for the Food and Drug Administration (FDA) when that agency failed to issue prompt warnings about the possible harmful consequences to women taking birth control pills. Research then being conducted indicated that the use of oral contraceptives could produce a variety of serious side effects. Dr. Pierce argued that the manufacturers of birth control pills should be required to put clear warning statements on their labels. When a year of debate within the agency failed to produce results, she resigned from the FDA in protest.

Not wanting to return to private practice, she entered the field of research and found that the work suited her. "In drug research you get results in a very short time," she told an interviewer recently. "You can tell whether a drug has no value or is worthwhile." Dr. Pierce was well-regarded by her fellow researchers. Co-workers at Ortho described her as a "fine scientist" and a "levelheaded" person.

During her first years at Ortho, a subsidiary of Johnson and Johnson, things went quite well for Dr. Pierce. The Raritan, New Jersey–based company was then shifting its emphasis from contraceptives and reproductive drugs, an area in which it had established a solid reputation, to the broader field of therapeutics. As part of this shift, Dr. Pierce was assigned to projects involving therapeutic drugs and, in 1973, was promoted to the position of director of medical research/therapeutics—a promotion which made her one of the top four staff members in Ortho's medical research department.

The trouble began early in 1975, when Dr. Pierce was assigned to a

*Unless otherwise specified, all statements by Dr. Grace Pierce quoted directly are taken from her sworn deposition given in 1977 when she initiated legal action against Ortho Pharmaceutical Corp.

project team that was investigating a new prescription drug, known generically as loperamide, for use in the treatment of acute and chronic diarrhea. Loperamide was to be given in liquid form to infants, children, and adults, particularly the elderly, who could not conveniently take medicine in solid form. (At Ortho, loperamide was known by the trade name Imodium and also as "Janssen's formula," a reference to the preparation developed by Ortho's European affiliate, Janssen of Belgium.)

One problem the loperamide team faced was eliminating the bitter taste of the drug so it would be palatable. To accomplish this, saccharin was added as a sweetener. There is still considerable controversy over the possible hazards to health that may—or may not—result from the use of saccharin and other artificial sweeteners. In some experiments, animals fed large dosages of saccharin have developed cancer. At the time Dr. Pierce and her colleagues were working on the loperamide project, the saccharin controversy spilled out of the laboratories and onto the pages of newspapers and magazines, and therefore was common knowledge.

(The debate still rages. In 1977, the FDA proposed a ban on the use of saccharin in foods, but Congress deferred the ban until 1979. No legislative action has been taken regarding other uses of saccharin, and there are, as yet, no federal standards restricting saccharin's use in drugs.)

What disturbed Dr. Pierce was the extremely high level of saccharin in the Ortho formula for loperamide. Each bottle of Imodium (loperamide) would have contained more than 40 times the amount of saccharin currently permitted by the FDA in a single 12-ounce can of diet soda. The other members of the research team shared Dr. Pierce's concern. The minutes of a meeting held on March 6, 1975, reveal that the team's toxicologist, Dr. C. D. King, believed that the saccharin level "in the Janssen preparation is too high and questioned using saccharin sodium at any level in the product." At the conclusion of the March 6th meeting the team expressed unanimous agreement that the Janssen formula—which was already being sold in Europe—was "not suitable for use in the United States."

Throughout the month of March, the project team continued to send memos to Ortho's management, restating its position on the Janssen loperamide formula and noting that an alternative formula, using sugar or smaller amounts of saccharin, could be developed in about three months. On March 26, the team issued an "Initial Status Report" urging reformulation of the Janssen preparation as a necessary step before "clinical testing and ultimate sale in the United States."

Because of this strong team disapproval of the Janssen Imodium formula, Dr. Pierce believed that the request to change the makeup of the drug would be swiftly approved. "I didn't think there would be any problem," she later recalled, "as reformulation would be an improvement on the product. It was a routine decision."

Dr. Pierce's optimism was soon shattered. Towards the end of March, a representative of the Janssen firm visited Ortho's New Jersey offices for the purpose of discussing the Imodium project. The Janssen representative met with Dr. Sam Pasquale, the executive director of Ortho's medical research department, and other company executives (although the record is unclear on this point). Immediately following this meeting, on March 28, a decision was reached to proceed with the testing and marketing of the Janssen formula and a plan of action was outlined in a memo.

Once again Dr. Pierce and her project co-workers demurred. The second part of the March 28th memo contains a listing of several "problem areas" encountered by the Imodium project team. The memo goes on to state: "The presence in the drop formulation of 17.5 mg. of saccharin sodium per milliliter represents a potential problem, as FDA may not permit the use of a product with saccharin present at this level. By comparison, FDA permits 15.8 mg. per fluid ounce as a sweetener (approximately 3% of the level currently being employed in Imodium drops)." Because of this and other problem areas, the team members expressed their "reluctance to 'lock into' the Janssen formulation of pediatric drops as the dosage form of choice."

Shortly afterward, a research associate who was a member of the project team submitted a memo to Dr. H. Weintraub, the chairman of the team, suggesting that the March 28th memo be revised to more accurately reflect what actually took place. The research associate wanted the record to state "very specifically" that the meeting with the Janssen representative, which led to the adoption of the plan of procedure for completing the Imodium project, "did not include the team as a whole or any individual member of the team." Furthermore, the five items contained in the plan of action had not been agreed to by the members of the team, but were, in fact, "directives that were given to the team" by higher authority.

On April 7, Dr. Pierce wrote a letter to Dr. Weintraub with her own suggested revisions for the minutes of the March 28th meeting. She requested that the following statement be included in the record: "It would be difficult to justify medically and legally our position of hastening into clinical trials with a questionable formulation when preliminary work in Pharmaceutical Development indicates a more acceptable formulation will be available very soon."

Dr. Pierce's position received further support from Dr. C. D. King, the project team's toxicologist. On April 10, in response to a request from the team chairman, Dr. King submitted a written summary of his objections to the Janssen formulation. The toxicologist noted that sodium saccharin caused bladder tumors, both benign and malignant, in laboratory test animals and that there is a "latent period of 17 years before the tumors become a clinical problem"—so that a "slow carcinogen" like saccharin might cause harm over a long period of time before the damage became apparent. "Therefore," Dr. King concluded, "any intentional exposure of any segment of the human population to a potential carcinogen is not to the best interest of public health or the Ortho Pharmaceutical Corporation. We do not have to market a formulation with high levels of saccharin; we do have an alternative approach."

But Ortho's management had already made a firm decision to proceed with the development of Janssen's loperamide formula. Just why the company was determined to continue with a drug its own research team questioned is a matter for conjecture. Dr. Pierce believes the company had set a firm deadline to get Imodium out on the market and therefore was unwilling to take any action that would upset the schedule. "The marketing people can go off half-cocked sometimes," she told a newspaper reporter. "They think millions of dollars are waiting to fall in their laps, promotions are to be had, careers to be made."

Ortho, for its part, has consistently maintained that its version of loperamide was not a health hazard. Company officials concede that a full bottle of the medication, under the Janssen formulation, would have contained a high level of saccharin; but they argue that the amount of saccharin in the dosage prescribed for a 24-hour period was less than is found in a single can of diet soda—and thus fell within FDA guidelines.

In any event, Dr. Pierce continued to hold out for a reformulation of the drug. However, under pressure from company management, her research team colleagues began to waver. There came a point when, as Dr. Pierce observes, "it became politically inadvisable to go against the order." By mid-April of 1975, several of the team members decided that it was expedient to go along with the company's directives. At a project team meeting held on April 18, a majority of the members voted "to proceed with due haste as 'Priority No. 1'" with clinical testing of the questionable Janssen formula.

Three days after this meeting Dr. Pierce wrote a memo to the members of the project team reaffirming her own position. "I did not and do not now agree with the majority decision in this matter," she stated. "In spite of the existing controversial evidence as to the ultimate safety of saccharin for human consumption, it is my strong opinion that justification for contemplating use or for requesting FDA permission to use the Janssen drop formulation is not evident. I respectfully request, in the interest of proceeding reasonably with this very worthy project, that an alternate formulation with no saccharin, or as low in saccharin as possible, be used."

In the weeks that followed, Dr. Pierce tried to resolve her differences with the company by suggesting what she felt were reasonable options. One proposal she made involved sending the drug to an outside panel of experts for an impartial review. In lieu of that, she suggested that the Janssen formula might be submitted to the FDA for discussion and comment. According to Dr. Pierce, both proposals were turned down.

As the only physician on the project team, Dr. Pierce felt she had a special responsibility beyond that of the other researchers. It would be her job to set up and monitor the tests on humans to determine what the drug did, what reactions people had to it, and, in general, how safe and effective it was. Her role would include explaining the drug's properties to other physicians and then supervising them as they dispensed the drug to test subjects. This special role, and the burden it placed on her, is underscored in the following exchange during the taking of her deposition.

QUESTION: Was there any particular judgment that you as the one doctor on that team had to make?

DR. PIERCE: I had to be sure that the research being done, or would be done, was in accordance with good medical ethics. I had to be sure that there would be no harm done to the people that would receive the drug. . . .

QUESTION: Was it therefore a unique position that a doctor had, an M.D. had, on that team?

DR. PIERCE: Yes. I had a special role to fill.

QUESTION: When the directives came through that your team was to proceed on the loperamide formulation, in your opinion were the other members of the team qualified to make a judgment on its harmful or nonharmful effects on human beings?

DR. PIERCE: They did make a judgment.

QUESTION: I am just asking you—in your opinion, did you believe that they were qualified?

DR. PIERCE: In a very limited way.

QUESTION: But was it a different way from your qualification?

DR. PIERCE: My responsibility went further than theirs . . . in that I would be responsible for seeing that the drug actually was given to humans. They didn't get involved in that, to that extent.

Early in May 1975, Dr. Pierce informed her superiors at Ortho that, as a matter of conscience, she could not be a party to human testing of the Janssen loperamide formula. A few days after she made her position known, company management reacted by removing her from the loperamide project. Under the circumstances, the company's action was understandable, but Dr. Pierce rejected Ortho's subsequent assertion that she was taken off the project because it was her desire not to do any further work on the loperamide formula. In her deposition, Dr. Pierce maintained that she wanted to change the formula and proceed with the work. "I wanted to be on that project but I didn't want to take that high saccharin formula out to the clinical practice," she stated. "I could not ethically take that out and give it to children."

On May 14, Dr. Pierce was called into the office of Dr. Sam Pasquale who, as Ortho's executive director of medical research, was her immediate superior. Dr. Pasquale accused her of irresponsibility, lack of judgment, and conduct unbecoming a director. He also told her that her level of productivity was unacceptable and that she had demonstrated an inability to cooperate with Ortho's marketing staff.

To these general criticisms, Dr. Pasquale added a list of specific complaints. He criticized Dr. Pierce for wasting company funds by taking a research associate on what he termed a needless field trip to Alaska, although company records reveal that the trip was approved by the vice president in charge of research—Dr. Pasquale's superior. Dr. Pierce was further admonished for having stayed too long at a medical conference in San Antonio, Texas. Again the record shows that she was directed to attend the conference by Dr. Pasquale, that she attended all sessions as directed, and that she received no instructions to cut short her stay before the conference was over.

At the end of the meeting, Dr. Pasquale informed Dr. Pierce that because of her "irresponsible behavior," she was going to be demoted. Furthermore, she was to be taken off all therapeutic drug projects. She was instructed to choose other projects that she would like to work on.

Up until that time, Dr. Pierce had worked harmoniously with Dr. Pasquale and had never been criticized by him. She left the meeting badly shaken. "I really didn't believe it," she reported later. "It's the first time during my career in industry that I've cried."

Early in June, Dr. Pierce went on vacation. Shortly after her return, on June 16, she was summoned to another meeting with Dr. Pasquale, who reiterated his earlier criticisms of her. In addition, he now accused her of having gone on vacation without notifying him. Dr. Pierce pointed out that back in February she had requested permission to attend the European Rheumatology Congress to be held in Helsinki, Finland, in June, because of certain research work she was doing at Ortho. She noted that her request was never answered, and that since early reservations were required, she went ahead and made plans. However, before leaving for Helsinki, she informed Dr. Pasquale's office of her vacation plans—being unable to speak to him directly because he was unavailable (he reportedly was giving testimony at a trial). It was also noted that although she conducted business for the company at the Helsinki conference, consulting with a Finnish physician on behalf of an Ortho colleague, she bore the entire cost of the trip herself.

Dr. Pasquale did not respond directly, but instead asked again which projects in the medical research-reproduction field she might want to pursue. In her deposition, Dr. Pierce claimed she replied that since Dr. Pasquale was the director, he "should decide where he believed I would best be suited. Upon asking with whom I would work, he didn't know for sure, but he told me I would be demoted, perhaps to associate director, and may or may not work with one or another research associates." Dr. Pasquale then told her that the company's top executives, including Ortho's president and its vice president of research, considered her unpromotable, and that he shared their opinion.

Dr. Pierce left this meeting convinced that she had no future at Ortho. "I went home . . . thinking about this, what he had said, the way things were going at Ortho," she later stated, "and he seemed to be just repeating what he had told me in the middle of May. It was almost like a canned speech, and I felt that there was no point in continuing, and I drafted my resignation that evening at home. . . ."

The following morning, June 17, 1975, Dr. Pierce submitted her letter of resignation, which stated in part: "Upon learning in our meeting of June 16, 1975, that you believe I have not acted as a director, have displayed inadequacies as to my competence, responsibility, productivity, inability to relate to marketing personnel, that you, and reportedly Dr. George Brun, vice president of research and development, and Mr.

Vern Willaman, president of Ortho Pharmaceutical, consider me to be nonpromotable, and that I am now or soon will be, demoted, I find it impossible to continue my employment with Ortho."

Dr. Pierce later stated that she believed that Ortho's offer of alternate projects was insincere, and that the company's intent in demoting her and accusing her of incompetence was both to punish her and to pressure her into resigning. When questioned by an Ortho attorney during deposition proceedings, this exchange took place:

QUESTION: Why did you feel there was no point in continuing?

DR. PIERCE: Well, I explained before. They had asked me to do something that I couldn't accept on ethical grounds and for that I was being punished.

QUESTION: And the punishment, in your mind, was being reassigned from one position to another one yet undetermined?

DR. PIERCE: What would you think?

Ortho disputes Dr. Pierce's account of the events leading up to her resignation. The company contends that the physician was not demoted but merely reassigned to other projects in her field. In support of their position, company officials point out that Dr. Pierce suffered no reduction in her $46,000-a-year salary. The company further maintains that her resignation was the result of "certain ongoing employment problems totally unrelated to loperamide, and her personal dissatisfaction at not having received a promotion long before the loperamide issue."

Not long after her resignation, Dr. Pierce decided to take legal action against Ortho. On May 6, 1977, she filed suit against the company to recover damages resulting from the termination of her employment. In her complaint, Dr. Pierce asserted that because of Ortho's actions, she had sustained damage to her professional reputation, disruption of her career, loss of salary, as well as seniority and retirement benefits, and had suffered physical and mental distress.

In December 1977, Ortho filed a motion for summary judgment—in effect, a dismissal of the case—on the grounds that, under common law, where no contract of employment exists between employer and employee, the employment is at the will of either party and may be terminated at any time, with or without justification. Since Dr. Pierce was an employee "at will," it made no difference whether her resignation was voluntary or induced. Under the "at will" rule, her employment could be terminated at the discretion of the company.

In a brief filed in opposition to Ortho's motion for summary judgment, Dr. Pierce's attorney, Ruth Russell Gray, argued that the "at will" rule should not apply in a situation where someone is acting to uphold professional ethics, since the public interest is involved and "a ruling in such a case as this . . . can affect professionals, not just physicians, anywhere in this state and possibly in the United States." By its actions, Ortho had effectively demanded that Dr. Pierce should act in a manner that violated "the ethical standards by which she was governed as a physician."

The brief noted also that courts in other states had modified the common law rule regarding "at will" employment in cases where public policy had been contravened—for example, employee firings that violated statutes prohibiting discrimination on the basis of sex, race, or age. Dr. Pierce, it was argued, was acting to uphold federal and state regulatory schemes concerning the development, production, and marketing of drugs. "She was the one person between the regulatory schemes and human use of the product and the person to see that the purpose of said schemes were fulfilled."

Following a hearing on the motion for summary judgment in January 1978, a New Jersey Superior Court judge ruled in favor of Ortho— on the basis of New Jersey's firm adherence to the common law principle that an employee without a contract may be fired at will. However, in rendering his decision, the judge observed: "Now it may be that public policy will develop to a degree that professionals, even though employees at will, will be permitted to resist what they consider to be a professionally unsound and unethical decision without fear of demotion or discharge." But he added that a trial court was not the place to make that determination.

Dr. Pierce immediately appealed the lower court ruling. On March 6, 1979, the Appellate Division of New Jersey's Superior Court reversed the decision by the lower court and sent the case back for a trial "on all of the issues raised by the pleadings." This was the first time that a New Jersey court had allowed a case of this nature to be tried on its merits.

In setting the stage for what could prove to be a landmark case, the appellate court took note of the fact that in recent years, courts in nearly a dozen states had permitted exceptions to the employment-at-will rule in cases where the employee's action was made necessary by violations of public policy. "This new doctrine," stated the court, "seems particularly pertinent to professional employees whose activities might involve violations of ethical or like standards having a substantial impact on matters of public interest, including health and safety." The court stated that the time might be at hand for New Jersey courts to rule on the ethics issues.

To avoid a flood of unwarranted litigation, the appellate court stressed that exceptions to the at-will rule must be restricted to those cases "involving truly significant matters of clear and well-defined public policy." In the case of Dr. Pierce, the court observed that the question of whether she resigned or was in effect discharged was "so intertwined with that relating to whether a public policy exception to the at will rule governing wrongful discharge should be adopted and applied that it is desirable that both issues be tried and determined at a plenary hearing."

It may be some time before the legal issues raised by this case are resolved. In the meantime, Dr. Pierce is trying to reconstruct her life. After leaving Ortho she attempted to get another job in the drug research field. She soon discovered that none of the other pharmaceutical companies would touch her. "I have to think the Ortho problem has something to do with it," she told a newspaper reporter. "I don't think the fact that you've sued your employer is a plus on your curriculum vitae." Dr. Pierce has resumed work as a clinical physician and is gradually establishing a private practice.

Whether or not Dr. Pierce wins a victory in court, she can claim a victory of sorts in her fight against Ortho's loperamide formula. In the wake of her departure, the company decided not to proceed with testing and marketing of the drug formulation. Company officials have not been specific about the reasons for the change in policy, stating only that the liquid formula proved to be "inconvenient to patients." In its place, a syrup mixture was substituted.

In spite of the difficulties of the past few years—the loss of employment in the field of her choice, the financial hardship as her income slipped to half of what it had been, and the emotional strain of a prolonged court battle—Dr. Pierce says she is not bitter. Rather she is "sorely disappointed" at the way Ortho treated her. She remains firm in her belief that she acted properly. "I know my decision not to give the drug to anyone was the right thing," she says. "I sleep well at night."

# Warning an Auto Company about an Unsafe Design

## Frank Camps

At the precise moment when the first Pinto
prototype smashed into the barrier at the Ford
testing grounds, the course of my career, as a senior
principal design engineer, and my life were changed.
I didn't know it then, of course, but that car would
send me on my own personal collision course with
the Ford Motor Company. The windshield failure
that occurred that day in July 1970 was repeated
many times that summer and in the following
months and years. My problem was that I was
directed to "forget" about failures by such devious
means as the subtle manipulation of documents and
crash data. I was instructed to inform the federal
government only of our successful test crashes—and
not the many failures.

   In those early days of Pinto testing, Ford's
management was adamant that the vehicle be

certified to comply with Federal Standards without delay—no questions asked—to meet the challenge of Volkswagen and the up-and-coming Japanese imports: Honda, Toyota, and the like. But because of the high number of test failures, we could not certify that the Pinto had passed the windshield retention test (Federal Motor Vehicle Safety Standard #212) and this led to desperate measures by corporate management. Orders came down from the Glass House (our in-house term for Ford's headquarters) to certify the Pinto at all costs—even if it meant changing long-standing procedures.

Customarily, the engineering analysis of a crashed vehicle brings out areas of design deficiencies that are corrected with a methodical, well-planned approach. Once the barrier crash sequence is concluded, management equates crash results with weight and cost factors to determine what course to follow. Not so for the Pinto. In this case, we were to use a fix-it-with-a-Band-Aid approach because management ruled at the inception of the program that to be competitive this vehicle must weigh no more than 2,000 pounds and cost no more than $2,000.

These criteria were inviolable and became a corporate-wide mandate for conformity. Consequently, we in the engineering department were forced to live with the design we had, whether or not we felt it was adequate. Reductions in weight and cost were acceptable; but additions were not to be considered, nor requested, under penalty of high-level censure. Therefore, we were permitted to make design changes that would reduce the strength of a component, but we could not take any action that would increase it; we could eliminate certain critical components not readily visible to the customer, but we could not add components because of the cost-weight limitations. We could use cheaper materials, but we could not add more expensive materials. The simple fact was that we were already tooled for production before our certification testing program began. Any substantive design changes would have jeopardized Ford's production schedule.

To meet federal safety standards concerning windshield retention we came up with a clever engineering ploy. We intentionally channeled some of the kinetic energy generated in the crash away from the windshield and transmitted that energy via the driveshaft to the differential housing, causing contact with the gas tank. The corporate reasoning was sound. Windshield retention was a federally mandated area of certification. Fuel system integrity, at that time, was not.

Let unsuspecting customers beware. Our main purpose as Ford employees was to increase corporate profits. (When asked by *Look* magazine, in 1968, to cite the biggest problem in the Ford Motor Company,

Henry Ford II responded: "That's easy—making more money.") As long as we were able to certify retention of the windshield, what was so important about the fuel system? What problem could it cause in the gas tank? No one gave any serious thought about potential hazards until years later, when Pinto gas tanks began exploding on impact in traffic accidents. Management's decision not to correct this weakness has, in recent years, come back to haunt the company in courtrooms across the country. In short we were forced to indulge in poor engineering practices, and had to assume responsibility for components we knew were marginal in design—or worse.

In my position as principal design engineer, I became a part of the Ford scheme. I was expected to be loyal to the company's policies and to ignore my own uneasiness about the safety of the cars we were approving. It did not take long before I came to the realization that company loyalty meant different things to different people. After the first few test crashes, a decision was made to deviate from standard test crash procedures, which had been used in approximately 1,600 previous tests. In the past, dummies simulating driver and passengers were always employed in safety tests. However, Pinto test crashes were to be conducted with *no dummies* aboard—not even a dummy driver. (Have you ever seen a driverless car?) Neither before nor since has Ford used this method of achieving federal certification. It was an unholy means to achieve what corporate management regarded as a justified end— getting the vehicle on the road to challenge the competition.

Of course, with no dummies in the car and by stripping the vehicle to its minimum weight, the Pinto was finally certified. But at what cost? We at Ford suffered untold damage to our reputation; the company was recently censured by the Supreme Court of Illinois for lying and holding back evidence. (The Illinois court, in upholding a lower court award of $678,000 in damages to the survivors of a crash, stated: "We cannot condemn too severely the conduct of Ford Motor Company. It gave false answers to interrogatories under oath. It secreted evidence damaging to its case.") Ford is currently spending millions of dollars in judgments and out-of-court settlements, and it has also experienced adverse media exposure because of the irresponsible actions it took in the 1970–72 series of Pinto tests. Unfortunately, I was an accomplice to those actions.

My concern about the on-the-road safety of the cars we were testing really began with the removal of the dummies from the test cars on July 18, 1970—only two weeks after the first test failure on July 6. The uneasiness I felt intensified when we came up with the ploy to divert the energy generated in a crash away from the windshield by directing it through the driveshaft to the gas tank. All of this took place early in our tests of the Pinto and some people might reasonably ask why I waited more than two years—until early 1973—before putting my concerns in writing. The answer is simple: I was afraid of losing my job. Bear in mind that I had three children, a wife suffering from multiple sclerosis, and a mortgage to worry about, so I could not afford to be out of work. I had already placed myself in sufficient jeopardy by my spoken attacks on the unorthodox testing methods being used and I was worried that a written memo to my superiors might put an abrupt end to my career at Ford.

During that long period of testing, which stretched from months into years, the Pinto continued to be a problem car, although the vehicle became somewhat more stable in crash situations. I vividly recall one series of crashes in October of 1971, when, over a period of 15 days, we barrier-crashed seven Pinto two-door models. The first five failed to meet minimum windshield retention standards. Then, late one Saturday night, by the manipulation of weights and assembly techniques, we succeeded in getting two vehicles to measure up to federal standards. And what about the five that failed? They were swept under the rug by being labeled "developmental tests," while the two that passed were submitted as federal certification cars.

At this point, let me say something about the windshield retention standard. While not considered as dangerous as fuel tank explosions, smashed windshields produce 11 percent of all serious and fatal head injuries suffered in car accidents. In addition, those injuries rated as minor in this category, and which usually receive less attention, often result in considerable human anguish. One should not overlook the massive psychological problems associated with injuries to the head— especially the long and difficult social rehabilitation associated with facial disfigurement.

The extent of the harm we had done hit me when I began reading about some of the accidents involving Pintos. A particularly shocking case occurred in California in 1972. A Pinto was struck in the rear, causing a gas tank explosion that quickly enveloped the car in flames. The driver of the Pinto, a 52-year-old woman, died of her burns; a 13-year-old boy named Richard Grimshaw, who was a passenger in the car, suffered burns over 90 percent of his body but survived. (You will recall that our success in obtaining windshield retention certification was at the expense of safe fuel tanks.) Since the accident, Grimshaw has had to undergo more than 50 operations and will probably have to endure another 20. On February 6, 1978, a California court awarded Grimshaw $128.5 million—the largest damages award in U.S. legal history. More recently, in 1980, the Ford Motor Company was indicted and tried for reckless homicide by an Indiana court in a case stemming from a 1978 Pinto crash and gas tank explosion that resulted in the deaths of three women. The jury found the company not guilty.

As for me, I went through my own form of agony—a crisis of conscience. Early in 1973, after weeks in which I was haunted daily by thoughts of the tragedies that might result from actions taken in my area of responsibility, I decided I could no longer remain silent. On February 18, I sent what was to be the first of many letters to Ford's management expressing my deep concern about the questionable procedures used in safety testing the Pinto. In that first letter, I wrote: "With each passing day it becomes clearer to me that our present way of life at Ford Motor Co. in regards to Federal Motor Vehicle Safety Standards is not only precarious but is at times in direct violation of the law." After pointing out that I faced the dilemma of either serving the best interests of the Ford Motor Company or submitting to the directives of my immediate superiors, I charged that "certain members of management are totally aware of violations of federal law as they relate to windshield strength and retention and have willfully and knowingly suppressed this information." I concluded by stating that I did not wish to be "made the scapegoat for the questionable integrity of others."

Although I had previously made my views known in conversations with my immediate supervisors, I now felt that I had to put my feelings on paper so that there would be a permanent record of my concern. At about this time, the concept that negligence in design is a basis for liability was taking hold in legal circles, and I was fearful of the consequences. Therefore, I wrote to management in order to allay my fears that at some future date I would be held personally liable for a Pinto fatality, as well as to assure myself that I had done whatever I could to abide by Public Law 89-563, section 102, which informs me that as a citizen and as an engineer I must take care "that the public is protected against unreasonable risk of accidents occurring as a result of the design, construction, or performance of motor vehicles and is also protected against unreasonable risk of death or injury to persons in the event accidents do occur."

I was keenly aware of my participation in the federal certification process. Proof of that involvement is contained in my annual performance appraisals for the years 1971, 1972, and 1973. These documents specify my involvement in the design of the Pinto, as well as citing that vehicle as the only one requiring a recertification program to achieve federal compliance.

It was subsequent to my many letters to management that I found in my 1973 appraisal a general downgrading of factors relating to my performance. My concern about safety was duly noted, but with different results than I had anticipated. The punitive action was beginning; ultimately it would lead to my being demoted to a position that did not involve vehicle testing. Refusals on my part to concur with management's appraisal of my work resulted in a steady decrease in involvement in the normal activities of a senior principal design engineer. I was excluded from design reviews with superiors; I was not included in various management development programs; and I was shuttled from one inconsequential job to another.

In other words, my punishment was to be banished to a corporate purgatory where all manner of disbelievers, boat rockers, and whistle blowers reside. But as I see it, the expression "blowing the whistle" describes a situation where an individual exposes wrongdoing or chicanery that another person, or a corporation, is indulging in. Therefore, "blowing the whistle" seems to me to be worthy of something other than exile.

During 1974, I participated in 11 meetings with members of Ford management in an attempt to resolve matters that troubled me. Finally, on December 1, 1974, I was demoted from my position as a design engineer with responsibilities that included compliance with Federal Standards No. 118 (Power Windows), No. 205 (Moveable Glass), No. 212 (Windshield Retention), and No. 217 (Bus Window Retention), to a position totally uninvolved with any federal standard compliance. The official reason given for my reassignment was that Ford was making a concerted effort to reduce the number of management personnel and thus to effect cost savings. These cost-saving measures were made necessary, according to management, by the nationwide recession. There are two reasons why I feel the demotion was purely punitive. First, although I was reduced from Grade 10 to Grade 9, I remained a member of management; second, my salary was not reduced.

During 1975, I continued to pursue my questioning of management based on my naive belief that no matter how powerful one's position in a corporation may be, no official entrusted with enforcing the laws (both federal and corporate) can violate those laws and go unpunished. Throughout 1975 and 1976 there were more meetings, more letters, and more frustrating disappointments. The high point of 1975 for me occurred when, after months of delays, I met in October with Jack Eckhold, the Director of Safety for the Ford Motor Company. Mr. Eckhold was gracious and disarming, but when we parted after two hours of discussion, he escorted me to the door with the final comment: "Mr. Ford does not take too kindly to 'whistle blowers,' " and added that it would be prudent for me to keep my mouth shut. Otherwise I might find myself out of a job.

Ironically, early in 1976, Henry Ford II issued Policy Letter C-3, entitled "Standards of Corporate Conduct," a clear and concise codification of Ford's response to illegality and improper behavior within the organization itself. The letter opened with these observations:

"To succeed and even to survive, Ford Motor Company must have the trust and confidence of its many publics. A good reputation is a priceless business asset that can be earned only through consistently trustworthy behavior.

"In recent months, the reputations of some of the largest and best-known American companies have been tarnished by exposure of illegal, unethical or questionable acts of members of management. We can be sure, as a result, that all companies will be watched more closely and held to higher standards."

Mr. Ford then emphasized that "particular care should be taken to act legally in those areas where the law is evolving rapidly. . . . Among those areas are . . . vehicle safety and emissions. . . . When in doubt, you should consult with the Office of General Counsel."

I had waited years for those words to appear in print. I felt that I was vindicated. It seemed clear that all I had to do was contact the Office of the General Counsel and I would receive an open, honest appraisal of the issues. In my naiveté, I had hoped and assumed that the counsel's office would review the facts and make objective determinations within our corporate structure. I know now I misjudged those persons charged by Ford with this responsibility. The delays of the previous years were child's play when compared to the professional procrastination that took place in my dealing with the prestigious Office of the General Counsel. On June 10, 1976, I sent a detailed memo to the general counsel's office, which contained the following statements:

"Based on Mr. Ford's letter of December 9, 1975, in which he discusses 'Standards of Corporate Conduct' and on the availability of the 'open door' avenue of appeal . . . I wish to once again voice my views regarding questionable decisions in Federal Motor Vehicle Safety Standard compliance made by members of Body and Electrical Product Engineering management during 1972–73. . . .

"I suggest that during the past three years, while endeavoring to bring these irregularities to the attention of upper management, I have been misled and misinformed by my supervisors, the BEPE Personnel Relations Office and the Corporate Safety Office. I further suggest that they have indulged in discrimination, intimidation, and collusion in their efforts to demean my image by their misuse of the management appraisal document and that these actions contributed to my reduction in grade. . . .

"If these types of retaliatory measures are to be one's reward for attempting to protect the 'public trust and confidence' of the Company Mr. Ford feels is so necessary to maintain the best interest of the Corporation, I am keenly disappointed in the corporate 'open door' policy as practiced at the middle management level. I am shocked at the deceit and intimidation used to abort any real attempt to objectively review the facts which are clearly supported by existing corporate records. . . ."

I was finally granted two meetings with officials there, but when I put the facts before them, I was carefully led down one garden path after another. They offered me only profuse apologies and shallow excuses for their not being able to hold additional meetings. Once again, I had been too trusting. Between July and December of 1976, no fewer than six meetings were cancelled for one reason or another. On February 14, 1977, I made one final attempt at seeking redress within the company when I asked Mr. James M. McNee of the general counsel's office if he had any intention of meeting with me again. He replied by note (which I still have), stating that arrangements would be made and that I would hear from him. I never did.

Shortly afterward, I wrote another letter to Ford management. Once more I expressed my concern about "questionable engineering judgments." My complaint, however, went beyond that of a design engineer to the broader issue of my treatment as an employee. I concluded by stating: "I am sure there are still those who confuse my dissent with disloyalty and my patience with weakness. To those persons I say this: if I were disloyal, this letter would have been directed to areas outside the corporate structure; if I were weak I would not have exhibited the tenacity to pursue this course for the past five years."

Nothing came of this letter and, during the months that followed, I agonized over what I could do to get the attention of management. I decided finally that further appeals to management, like my earlier ones, were likely to fall on deaf ears. My only alternative, it seemed, was action in the form of litigation in which I would ask the court for protection from personal liability in accidents arising from windshield failures. I also charged discrimination on job assignments because of my "boat rocking" and my age.

In 1978, I resigned from the Ford Motor Company, convinced that I had come to the end of the road in my career there. I am currently working three days a week as a consultant to American Motors on a military vehicle program involving jeeps of different sizes. In American Motors, I feel that I have found a more open-minded employer. I am permitted to freely take time off to spend with my ailing wife, when her condition requires my presence, and I am also allowed to take time off to pursue my other occupation as a technical consultant to attorneys involved in product liability cases.

My litigation against Ford is still pending. In July 1979, attorneys representing Ford took my deposition. They were most anxious to find out about my consultant activities in the area of product liability—including the names of attorneys who were using me as a consultant. On the advice of my own attorney, V. Paul Donnelly, I refused to answer any questions involving my work as a consultant in this field. We are now awaiting further developments in the case.

In the meantime, I feel I have been partially vindicated in that the Pinto windshield-retention system was subsequently revised to conform to a concept I originally proposed in June 1972. However, this design was not incorporated until the 1979 model year, with the unfortunate result that, since the introduction of the model, an estimated 915,000 subcompact Pinto station wagons have been put on the road with windshields that failed to meet federal standards. (In addition, there are 2½ million sedans that exhibit borderline retention.)

My experience at Ford also taught me a disheartening lesson about the distorting effects that the company can have on the individual worker. After I brought my concerns to the attention of the Office of the General Counsel, I sought among my co-workers—as did Diogenes—an "honest man" to stand with me against management. I thought I had found one or two persons who would support my claims. But my hopes were quickly dashed. I discovered that many colleagues, who previously shared my views, had received promotions in grade and substantial salary increases by following orders. Needless to say, they were no longer interested in voicing their displeasure with company safety-testing procedures. It is not surprising that a corporation with unlimited resources can buy or intimidate people into just "going along."

But why, after 25 years of service, did I choose to blow the whistle?

My answer is simple. I was being made the scapegoat for persons whose irresponsible actions were a potential threat to my personal integrity and my way of life. I strongly resented the attempt to place the onus on me for management's short-sighted decisions in the area of windshield retention, fuel system integrity, and beyond. As I wrote in my letter of June 6, 1975, to Mr. Eckhold: "When, at some future date, an unfortunate individual endures suffering as the direct result of an accident in one of the vehicles I have described, I want to feel that I did everything in my scope of influence to prevent such a tragedy. I also want to know that I did not contribute to another's misfortune by compromising my personal standard to do the best possible job from a standpoint of design, performance, and safety. Further, I want to feel that I did not jeopardize the integrity of the Ford Motor Company in the performance of those duties."

There are those in the company who would contend that, in exchange for the salary I received for 25 years, I was obliged to "follow the rules," however much they deviated from Ford's official "Standards of Corporate Conduct." But I see the story from another perspective. In 1953 I was recruited by Ford to contribute my engineering and design talent to a floundering, ill-managed corporation. Although I hesitate to place my name in the category of those like Ernest R. Breech and Lewis D. Crusoe—the two executives most responsible for the Ford Motor Company's resurgence in the post-World War II period—I, too, gave of my expertise and contributed my skills during those years of struggle to return our company to a position of prestige and profitability.

By the mid-sixties, we had made our mark; we were a weak second to General Motors—but second nevertheless—and a force to be reckoned with in the automotive industry. By then, I had reached the level of principal design engineer. I felt I had a substantial equity in the resurgence of our company. Not only had I given of myself on the job, but I had also shown my interest in Ford by my regular purchases of company stock. Therefore, I felt that I was not only an employee but also a part-owner. Because of my management responsibilities and my position as a stockholder, I felt I had both the right and the duty to express my feelings about corporate policy, especially in areas involving vehicle safety. However, when Ford did come of age, the fact that we oldtimers had infused the "spark" in the corporation was forgotten. The new ideal was to upgrade management with younger blood. The equity that I and many others had built up through long years of struggle in the formative process counted for very little.

Nevertheless, my performance levels remained high, as demonstrated by the above average and excellent ratings I received in the yearly management appraisals. There was no reason other than punishment for my demotion, no reason other than spite for the subsequent harassment and embarrassment I suffered at the hands of the company hierarchy. Whatever obligation I had to Ford was fulfilled by 25 years of hard work and steady performance. My attempt to bring the dangers of the Pinto vehicle to the attention of the public was not a disloyal act, but rather one designed to avoid tragedy—an act in the public interest. I did not turn away from Ford but in my own way I rose to its defense. I realize that most Ford executives probably would not see it this way. But I continue to firmly believe that the truly loyal employee is the one who helps to keep the company on the right track—producing a good product that is safe for the consumer to use.

# Conclusion: What Can and Should Be Done to Protect Whistle Blowers in Industry

## Alan F. Westin

The ten people whose stories have just appeared represent a pretty good cross section of corporate employees in the United States. They range in age from early thirties to early sixties. There are Easterners, Southerners, Midwesterners, and Westerners. Some are Democrats, some Republicans, and some Independents; in political philosophy, some are conservatives, some liberals, and some wholly apolitical. In terms of occupational positions, five of these people were in professional or technical posts, three had "line" jobs (production worker, secretary, and truck driver), one was in sales, and one was a research manager. Interestingly, none of them were crusaders or movement activists at the time they decided to speak out against their company's policies. None of these persons was a "poor performer" or had previously experienced difficulty in getting along with co-workers, supervisors, or customers. All were receiving good or superior ratings on the job before the issue arose that eventually led to their blowing the whistle.

The issues they raised were not general questions of business policy, on which management generally ought to be free to make the decisions, nor were they abstract questions of business ethics. In each case, it was alleged violations of law, serious breaches of safety, or potential dangers that were at stake. Dan Gellert, Leo Kohls, Bob Elliot, Peter Faulkner, Frank Camps, and Grace Pierce believed that the safety of workers, customers, or the public was being endangered. Cristine Colt and Adrienne Tompkins protested sexual discrimination forbidden by federal law. Joseph Rose and Arthur Suchodolski were outraged at the illegal-payment or false-reporting practices they believed their managements to be conducting. Each case involves the moral choice employees face when an employer directs them to continue doing things that either contribute further to a dangerous or illegal condition or leave it uncorrected.

With the possible exception of Peter Faulkner, these employees first raised the issue that concerned them with their supervisors or higher management before they went "public" to government agencies or the press. As a result, these cases cannot be dismissed as situations in which low-level supervisors did things that violated company policy and were unknown to middle or top management.

What is especially striking in these accounts is the identical way that these employees, slowly and in disbelief, came to realize that nothing was going to be done to correct the wrongdoing that they had identified and had brought to management's attention. Each had been warned to let it drop, to go along with management's judgment and get back to work. Some were offered inducements of salary increases and favorable job opportunities if they cooperated. Others received threats of reprisal and dismissal if they didn't shut up. All went home and pondered what continued dissent would mean to their careers and personal lives. Each also considered what a willingness to be silent would mean to their consciences, their sense of professional integrity, or their own safety at work. Each chose to go on with the protest, and, eventually, to become a whistle blower. Of the ten whistle blowers in this book, only one was able to win reinstatement, and only two others have secured partial damages in court for what happened to them. The other seven have been unable to obtain reinstatement, damages, or vindication of their professional reputations.

## Summing Up the Implications of These Cases

As we begin the 1980s, two basic judgments seem justified by the experiences of these and other whistle blowers of the past decade:

1. The harm that can be done to worker and public health, consumer safety, and the environment by corporate mistakes or disregard of law has grown so serious, and its future effects so awesome, that we need to improve the mechanisms of decision making within the corporation, to weigh risks and costs more effectively from the standpoint of the public interest. Greater internal-dissent and error-detection procedures are vital to such an improved process, along with a better early warning system to alert society at large to dangers *before* their consequences engulf us.

2. The internal and external protections of legitimate whistle blowing that began to be applied in the late 1970s are still very fragile and isolated blooms in a rocky organizational and legal soil. It is simply not enough that a few dozen companies out of 10,000 large enterprises have adequate employee-rights programs that affect whistle-blowing matters. As for the law, the opinions of the majority of courts in the 1970s make it clear that most judges are still uncomfortable with "public policy" exceptions to employer firing powers. Also most government agencies do not give enough help within a reasonable time to whistle blowers who have been the victims of reprisal actions.

My conclusion is that our society needs to rethink the current definitions of loyalty and dissent in corporate life. We must come up with a strategy that will apply a combination of new remedies to increase the protection of legitimate whistle blowing. And, we have to start discussing this issue with some urgency now, if we are to take the actions that the public interest requires for the 1980s and beyond.

## The Complexities to Be Considered in Framing New Policies

Having stated this conclusion, it may seem that this presents a relatively straightforward problem for American law and social policy: just create some new procedures to protect whistle blowers. But the problem is not at all simple. Consider the following factors that have to be taken into account in framing new public policies.

1. *Not all whistle blowers are correct in what they allege to be the facts of management's conduct, and determining the accuracy of whistle-blowing charges is not always easy.* Even though we presented ten examples where corporate employees seem to have been in the right, this is often not the case. If it were possible to collect all the instances of corporate-employee whistle-blowing charges in the United States in a given year and then determine how often managements were justified in their actions and the employees mistaken, my guess is that employers would deserve to win many of these disputes. This has been the experience under independent labor arbitration, when unionized workers challenge dismissals as not being for "just cause." It is also the experience when government employees have appealed to the courts to vindicate free-expression rights in government whistle-blowing cases. Putting the whistle to one's lips does not guarantee that one's facts are correct.

2. *There is always the danger that incompetent or inadequately performing employees will take up the whistle to avoid facing justified personnel sanctions.* Forbidding an employer to dismiss or discipline an employee who protests against illegal or improper conduct by management invites employees to take out "antidismissal insurance" by lodging a whistle-blowing complaint. Any new system to protect whistle blowers must find ways to deal with this possibility.

3. *Employees can choose some ways of blowing the whistle that would be unacceptably disruptive, regardless of the merits of their protest.* Suppose an employee at a chemical plant takes out an ad in the local newspaper that says, "My company is violating the law by polluting the town reservoir." Or suppose a black employee of the XYZ Corporation comes to work on the assembly line one day wearing a large button that says "XYZ is a Honkie Firm that Practices Racism against its Black Workers." Finally, suppose an automobile design engineer, without raising the issue with his supervisor or upper management, reports to the National Transportation Safety Board that he believes the gas tank of a new model just entering production will pose grave safety problems. These illustrations demonstrate that any system to protect rights of employee expression must consider the time, place, and manner in which an employee voices that dissent.

4. *Some whistle blowers are not protesting unlawful or unsafe behavior but social policies by management that the employee considers unwise.* When this is the case, should such an employee be entitled to remain on the job? In considering this, it helps to recall that whistle blowing can come in a wide

variety of ideological stripes. Most government and corporate whistle blowers have recently been people who are asserting liberal values when they call for changes in corporate policies. But in the late 1940s and early fifties, the most celebrated whistle blowers were persons leaking information to anti-Communist legislators or the press about allegedly "soft-on-communism" policies by members of the Truman administration or their private employers. It was Senator Richard M. Nixon who proposed legislation in 1951 to protect the jobs of such federal-employee whistle blowers if they revealed classified information about corruption or pro-Communists to congressional committees. At that moment, liberals and civil libertarians defended the need for autonomy and confidentiality in the Executive Branch, and deplored the totalitarian "informer" mentality being championed by the McCarthyites. This suggests that any policy protecting whistle blowers must reckon with the likelihood of shifting ideological directions among protesting employees, and consider how often society wants social policies to be determined in the private sector through whistle-blowing disputes.

5. *The legal definitions of what constitutes a safe product, danger to health, or improper treatment of employees are often far from clear or certain.* It usually takes years and many test cases before the courts and regulatory agencies define just what is required in a given situation. This leaves open a wide range of judgments and choices as to what is proper compliance activity. Until the law becomes clear, shouldn't management have the authority to select compliance strategies, since management bears the legal responsibility for meeting standards? This is especially true since the harsh realities of foreign business competition and rising production expenses create legitimate concerns for management about containing costs, including the costs of complying with government regulations. In addition, the jobs of millions of corporate employees, the well-being of local communities in which companies operate, and the strength of the national economy are all involved in the determination of reasonable risk-to-cost calculations.

6. *The efficiency and flexibility of personnel administration could be threatened by the creation of legal rights to dissent and legalized review systems.* If it becomes legally protected to challenge management policies and procedures and to appeal directives to outside authorities, this could lead to a flood of unjustified and harassing employee complaints. It could require personnel managers to document every action as a defense to possible litigation, and embroil managements in constant employee litigation. It could

also create an "informer ethos" at work that would threaten the spirit of cooperation and trust on which sound working relationships depend.

7. *There can be risks to the desirable autonomy of the private sector in expanding government authority too deeply into internal business policies.* Although democratic societies have a major interest in allowing private organizations to run their own affairs and to make their own personnel decisions, they insist that these private organizations are also subject to obeying the law. Having courts or government tribunals pass on the validity of a wide range of personnel decisions could give the government more authority to define loyalty and disloyalty for 80 million private-sector employees than would be desirable, and could also give government too much authority to control what products are produced and how they are manufactured.

This catalogue of institutional and social problems does *not* mean that we should abandon the effort to install new whistle-blower protections in the private sector. It does suggest that we need to be sensitive to the multifaceted aspects of the task, and to recognize that care now could save much regret later over the "unanticipated consequences" of a new policy.

Given the complexity of these issues, how do we begin? It always helps to start by making explicit the assumptions and value judgments that one holds, so that these can be weighed openly in the public debate over new principles, policies, and procedures.

## Some Assumptions to Frame the Discussion

I start by assuming that the private enterprise system will be with us for many years to come. There is no sign that the American public wishes to nationalize most of industry, and, indeed, denationalization is currently the agenda of many European nations such as Britain, France, and Italy. Even if nationalization were a viable option in American society, there is not the slightest sign that problems of whistle blowing disappear when government runs productive facilities or offices, or administers large work forces. Thus, new policies will have to be formulated for a large private-corporate sector, and one that will continue to be marked by significant diversity according to industry, size of firm, type of activity, management style, and other factors. Such policies will also need to take into account some important institutional difference between government whistle blowing—which involves misuse of public funds and perversion of the standards set by law for public officials—and corporate-employee whistle blowers who allege violations of the more limited legal regulations over the private sector. In addition, there are genuine issues of regulatory costs and of protection of the autonomy of private organizations for balance-of-power values in American society that need to have very careful attention, once the continuation of the private enterprise system is assumed.

I also assume that explaining corporate misconduct in terms of the personal morality or immorality of individual corporate managers represents a highly limited perspective. Few business executives deliberately seek to turn out cars that are defective, or to injure workers on the job, or to turn their local communities into poisoned environments. The real problem has been the frame of reference for business decisions and the reward structure of companies. These have simply not been brought into harmony with the new demands of public-protection laws of the 1970s.

While some companies have been notable for their adoption of an anticipative-management approach to social change, and have been innovative in formulating new policies to respond to changing public demands, the great majority of companies have been grudging at best in their compliance philosophy. Schooled in the pre-1970s era of "acceptable" race and sex discrimination, they had to be pushed each step of the way toward techniques of recruitment, training, employee-development, performance appraisal, and promotion that meet true merit-employment standards. Long used to assuming that any harm done to employees in the production process was an "accepted hazard" of employment, and that the long-term costs to employee health and family life should be paid by society, many managements have resisted adopting safe-workplace procedures to respond effectively to the health dangers that have been discovered.

The recently published account of General Motors in the 1960s, provided by one of its former top executives, John Z. De Lorean, shows a management so driven by the demand for profits that the strong objections of GM engineers about the safety of the Corvair were simply swept aside. "Management not only went along with [this position]," De Lorean reports, but it also "told the dissenters in effect to 'stop these objections. Get on the team, or you can find someplace else to work....'" Because of the manner in which top management decisions were made, De Lorean saw each executive being led to give "his individual approval in a group of decisions which produced the car in the face of serious doubts that were raised about its safety." Once that decision had been made, De Lorean explains, GM's management went to extraordinary lengths "to squelch information that might prove the car's deficiencies."[1]

Taking the long view of history, one might say that it is not surprising that the past 10–15 years have seen most managements unable or unwilling to change a system of closed decision making that stressed short-term profits and rewarded tough "can-do" managers. Creating change in such an environment required a combination of new forces to accompany the enactment of legislation: wide publicity of these issues in the mass media; a sustained demonstration of new public attitudes; clear proof of substantial harm being done to workers, customers, and communities; and opening up corporate decision-making processes to scrutiny and disclosure by regulatory agencies and courts. The fact that this challenge to management took place in years of serious recession, energy crisis, and increased foreign competition rather than in a period of economic and social stability also must have contributed to the slow corporate response.

While this is probably true in the long view, the central task for American industry and society alike in the 1980s is to find ways now to move corporate managements with greater effectiveness toward the new systems our public policy mandated. To do this, the organizational environment of corporate life obviously has to be changed to give much stronger support to policies that genuinely meet the new social demands for equal opportunity, employee rights, safe workplaces and products, and a livable environment. This requires building a positive commitment to such policies on the part of top corporate leaders.

One other group of assumptions should be noted as background for policy discussions. I assume that management should still have the right to organize and to direct the policies of the firm, and this includes the right to set rules and procedures for the employee workforce; this is, after all, the authority which makes those managers responsible in law to stockholders, to customers, and to society for the proper conduct of the organization. Similarly, employees should still have a general obligation to perform assigned duties satisfactorily and to follow all lawful directives of the management; this is, after all, what allows large organizations to pursue their objectives efficiently. But there are also several functional needs of modern complex organizations that have come to be increasingly recognized. Managements need the frank and freely expressed views of employees to achieve the best possible policies and to help police the faithfulness of company actions to policy directives. At the same time, the enterprise as a whole needs an efficient internal process by which the legally responsible officers can resolve disputes about the wisdom or legality of company policies. The more that corporations must operate in complex, risk-bearing environments, and in an era of rapidly changing regulatory standards, the more such a process of frank discussion and good conflict resolution is needed. Free expression and dissent in the contemporary corporation is not, therefore, a cosmetic matter of good public relations or a ploy to cool out grievances and avoid unionization. It is a vital way to ensure that management proposals and policies get the thorough, sometimes critical review they need if the company is to operate as a lawful and ethical entity.

## Three Types of Whistle-Blowing Situations

Based on these assumptions about the need to develop new policies to protect conscientious corporate dissenters in the eighties, how should our society proceed? The beginning of a new approach is to refine the categories we use to describe and judge whistle-blowing situations.

We should distinguish three kinds of conduct by management that employees may feel they are compelled to protest.

### 1. Clear Illegality

This covers breaches of law that—if the employee is correct in the facts alleged—would represent knowing and flagrant violation by company officials. This would include false reporting of test results to government agencies, bribery of government inspectors, illegal campaign contributions, false auditing reports, deliberate racial discrimination in hiring, deliberate dumping of forbidden chemicals in local water supplies, deliberate violation of labor laws, etc. The essence of this category is that the legal standards are clear, and management's violation is alleged to be knowing and deliberate. Both inside the company and in terms of outside review, charges of clear illegality ought to be given the highest priority in terms of hearing the employee, correcting the lawlessness, and shielding the employee from reprisals. "No one and no policy is above the law" should be the acknowledged spirit in which such issues are investigated and dealt with in an ethical company.

### 2. Potential Illegality or Danger

Given the growing network of detailed public regulation needed to protect worker health, consumer safety, public health, and the environment, there will be many situations—probably the majority of whistle-blowing events—in which an employee believes that a given product design, work process, or personnel practice is not in compliance with regulatory standards. In any well-run enterprise, management should be seriously concerned about such violations (to follow the law and avoid penalties for not doing so) and should welcome warnings by its own employees that regulations would not be met. But for all the reasons we have seen in this book—pressures of production schedules, competition, profit margins, management careers, and the like—supervisors, middle managers, and top management may all choose to ignore such warnings, or override them as unsound, citing "management's right to manage" as the ultimate justification.

In the great majority of daily situations, management's judgment may well be superior if the issues of potential illegality or danger have been foreseen and a specific issue subjected to full-dress examination at a high enough mangement level for the particular problem. But for situations where an employee or executive is still convinced that there is potential illegality or danger, company policy should provide a well-known and workable process that provides mechanisms for hearing and decision. When such a process is present, as we will discuss later in detail, the employee should have a duty in most cases to use that process before going to the public.

### 3. Business Social Policy

Corporations being rich and powerful institutions, an employee may become concerned over the fundamental morality of a management policy and its effect on our society. This can involve making a given product (nuclear power, for example), how the company invests its money (in South African industries), what social or political causes the company supports in advertising or contributions, and a host of other issues. Assuming that the company policy is not illegal, an employee protest first raises the issue of what is to be protected free speech on the part of employees. Clearly, corporate employees are entitled to the rights of free speech as citizens of a democratic society. At the same time, business is by law and social acceptance entitled to pursue lawful business activity even if some of its employees object to it, always subject to having the company's products rejected or its reputation tarnished if it does things that particular social groups or society at large feels to be morally wrong. The point of conflict obviously arises when an employee speaks out publicly against a lawful company policy on moral grounds and thereby harms the reputation and business advantage of the firm. Deciding what the law should do raises questions of the content of the speech, to whom it is addressed, how it is expressed, and other pivotal questions that will be discussed later in this chapter.

The value of distinguishing these three types of situations is that they help society to judge more clearly what is involved in a given whistle-blowing situation. Using these categories can also suggest the different kinds of internal mechanisms that company managements should have to handle each type of protest, and to help courts and other review agencies to define more concretely the respective responsibilities of employees and managers in a given situation.

Turning now to a discussion of what needs to be done, we take up the main arenas of possible action: (1) internal policies and procedures that management should institute; (2) mechanisms for outside review and action by governmental bodies and courts; and (3) the role that professional, public-interest, and employee-protection groups can play in whistle-blowing situations.

## New Management Policies and Procedures: The Inside Mechanisms

The single most important element in creating a meaningful internal system to deal with whistle blowing is to have top leadership accept this as a management priority. This means that the chief operating officer and his senior colleagues have to believe that a policy which encourages discussion and dissent, and deals fairly with whistle-blowing claims, is a good and important thing for their company to adopt. Executives of American business have to be convinced that such protection of dissent is, in both the short and the long run, important for their company's progress. They have to see such an approach as essential if their firms are to operate effectively in the risk-heavy environment of the 1980s, and to secure the best efforts of an increasingly rights-conscious workforce. They have to see it, in their own terms, as a moral duty of good private enterprise.

How this positive approach by top management can be applied to dissent and whistle blowing was discussed recently by Alexander B. Trowbridge at the Second National Seminar on Individual Rights in the Corporation. Mr. Trowbridge was then vice chairman of Allied Chemical Company, and is now president of the National Association of Manufacturers. As a former Secretary of Commerce during the Johnson administration, he had experience as a government administrator as well as a corporate executive. Mr. Trowbridge said:[2]

In today's world, the corporation must tolerate, perhaps even encourage, a considerable degree of free speech among its employees. It must do so not merely to avoid the charge it is muzzling its staff, but to assist management in policing the operations of a large, sometimes far-flung and often highly decentralized business. Are illegal practices being pursued in some part of the company's operations? Are the corporation's ethical standards being circumvented by certain managers? Is discrimination being practiced in the employment or promotion of blacks or women? Are unsafe or inferior products being sold to the company's customers?

The modern corporation must encourage the honest and concerned employee to blow the whistle on illegalities and actual malpractices. It must give the whistle blower access to the people who can change things. And it must protect him against recrimination. . . .

[But] systems and programs designed to protect employee rights can never provide the *whole* answer to the problem. Of equal or greater importance, it seems to me, is the organizational climate within the corporation. It must be one that fosters the development of discipline in response to strong leadership and yet creates an atmosphere in which the individual, when confronted with something clearly illegal, unethical or unjust, can feel free to speak up—and to bring the problem to the attention of those high enough up in the corporation to solve it.

Obviously, no company can create such a climate overnight. It requires time and the unwavering adherence of top management to the highest standards of fairness in dealing with all levels of employees. It requires management that will stand just as firm against the denial of an employee's rights as it will against the selfish abuse of those rights. It requires especially a dedication by management to principle rather than expediency, year in and year out, regardless of the urgency of the issue of the moment.

The creation of such a continuing attitude of responsibility, openness, and commitment on the part of top management is the first step in developing a meaningful internal policy. The next step is the drafting of principles and policy statements that apply management's intention throughout the company, and the communication of this policy to all employees. It is especially important not only that middle and line managers be informed about the policy, and given concrete training in its meaning and application, but also that adherence to such policy be built into the reward and penalty structure of management.

In a profit-oriented organization, ambitious managers know that their prospects, from annual bonus to promotions, are tied to profit-based appraisals by superiors. While each department within the company might have different ways of measuring the contribution to profit-making, one thing was usually clear in the 1950s and 1960s—complying with restrictive new laws or enhancing employee rights was not something for which a corporate manager got brownie points.

This reward system began to change in the 1970s. As fines and back-payment awards in equal employment opportunity cases began to reach sizable sums even for large corporations, and as similar sums were awarded in lawsuits or government proceedings involving pollution and product safety, many managements realized they had to build greater attention to these issues into the corporate reward system. At one major chemical company, a third of the annual bonus of the 200 top executives now depends on meeting company performance requirements in environmental and occupational health.[3] Many companies have adopted a similar practice in assessing the performance of managers in meeting EEO objectives. Such reward systems, if widely adopted in business, would give managers a greater stake in identifying and correcting defective products and policies, and this could make dissent by employees more "useful" to the executive corps itself.

Even the best drafted policy statements and management training programs will not resolve all the questions of illegal, dangerous, or improper conduct that might arise. There has to be a clear process of receiving complaints, conducting impartial investigations, defining standards of judgment, providing a fair-hearing procedure, and reaching the most objective and responsible decision possible. Such a procedure has to be fair both to the complaining employee and to company officials if morale is to be preserved and general confidence in management's integrity is to be the general expectation of the work force.

When collective bargaining contracts for unionized employees and their grievance machinery are not involved, the great majority of American corporations use three elements to handle employee complaints: the immediate supervisor; the personnel department; and some kind of "Open Door" appeal to management.[4] Many whistle-blowing issues involving personnel decisions (race and sex discrimination, sexual harassment, age discrimination, etc.) can and probably should be handled through this traditional chain of appeal. But the personnel department does not have the substantive skills or the authority within the company to handle issues of product design, dangerous work processes, environmental pollution, or other alleged violation of regulatory standards.

As it has traditionally been administered, the Open Door program of appeal to a plant manager, division head, or company chief executive has been more of a promise than an operating reality. The weakness in practice has usually been the absence of a well-publicized and easily accessible means to lodge an appeal; a well-staffed investigative system; a powerful enough commitment of time and attention by the chief executive officer to create a "without-fear-or-favor" approach to reaching decisions; and a publicized record of decisions that indicate enough rulings adverse to management to satisfy employee concerns for impartial judgment. IBM is an example of a company in which the conditions for effective use of the Open Door exist and could be applied in whistle-blowing situations.[5] But very few companies that I know of have such carefully administered Open Door programs.

A few companies, such as General Electric's Aircraft Frame Division, Control Data Corporation, Singer, and McDonald's, have created Ombudsmen programs that provide a single official to receive, investigate, and respond to employee complaints.[6] This can be an important forum for the employee who believes illegal or improper conduct is taking place, especially if the Ombudsman is an experienced executive who enjoys the open and determined support of the company's chief executive officer. For many situations, especially overzealousness by middle managers or violation of the company's own rules and ethical guides, the Ombudsman can be an effective resource. However, very few companies have adopted the Ombudsman technique so far. And, the problem with using the Ombudsman in some whistle-blowing situations is that the Ombudsman may not be able to deal effectively with a charge of illegal or improper conduct by a "line function" such as design, production, or sales. There is likely to be even greater difficulty when senior executives of the company are actively promoting this conduct as a company imperative.

In recognition of this problem, Citibank created a special procedure in 1980 that its employees can use when whistle-blowing issues arise.[7] While Citibank already had a Good Practices Committee of its Board of Directors, this was a general supervisory mechanism and not one specifically addressed to the whistle-blowing problem. Also, Citibank had experienced an employee complaint of alleged illegality that had drawn headlines in 1978–79.[8] Believing that a more explicit policy for receiving and reviewing complaints was needed, Citibank personnel set out to draft a new procedure to handle accusations by employees of questionable, unethical, or illegal practices, and one that would apply to Citibank's activities worldwide, not just in the United States. (Taking into account the diversity of laws and practices in the many countries in which Citibank operates proved the biggest difficulty, a Citibank executive noted. "If it had only been for the United States, we could have issued it a year ago."[9]

First, the policy requires each of Citibank's business units to communicate to employees the bank's existing guidelines on ethical standards and conflicts of interest, and its regular procedures for handling employee concerns over such matters. (These include a "Citiline" query program on management policies, special reviews by the personnel department, medical or counseling procedures, and direct complaint to management or audit officials.)

Second, the policy specifies that there can be "occasions when an employee may question or object to actions or decisions taken by the organization or by one or several individuals." This might involve actions that are viewed as being "illegal or against public interest, undermining the trust or rights of the organization's employees or customers," or "detrimental to the reputation, the profitability or the sound operations of the organization," such as "violations of corporate policies or practices" or "abuse or mismanagement of corporate resources, property, privilege, public influence or vested authority."

The code recognizes that an individual concerned about such matters "may feel personally affected by the situation or feel compelled to act on it as a matter of conscience. . . ." This could lead employees "to challenge decisions or actions, or to bring higher management's attention to what they feel is a questionable practice that has gone unheeded or unnoticed."

When this occurs, though existing procedures may still be used if the employee wishes, the code creates "a separate and distinct global corporate procedure for the internal disclosure and investigation of allegations of questionable practices." The reasons given for having such a system are an interesting blend of commendable idealism and practical management sense:

- to allow such concerns to surface constructively and without fear of retribution or alienation;
- to provide a focal point where matters of this nature can be initially analyzed, evaluated, and differentiated from others [and] steered through a coherent institutional framework designed to ensure impartiality, confidentiality, and thorough investigation;
- to exhaust internal channels of discussion and resolution and protect the organization and all affected parties from what may be unwarranted public attention;
- to ensure that our corporate commitment to integrity and respect for the individual is maintained in practice as well as spirit.

The process set up to handle such complaints calls for each business unit of Citibank to create "questionable practices" review mechanisms that provide for "prompt" investigation and resolution "without fear of retribution or alienation." Employees can also file their complaints directly with a central Committee on Good Corporate Practice in Citibank's New York corporate headquarters. The Committee decides whether to investigate the complaint itself or forward it to the head of personnel relations at the bank's New York offices. Provisions are made for interviewing and gathering information on complaints, decision by the chairman of the Committee alone, or the convening of the full Committee, and for timely communication of the final decision to all concerned parties.

As with Open Door policies, the effectiveness of Citibank's new policy will depend on the quality of the investigative, hearing, and decision processes, and the protection of employees who use it from "reprisal or alienation." But the promulgation of such a clear worldwide policy recognizing the importance of ethical practices and protection of employee conscience represents a model of what corporate management can do to ensure that good internal mechanisms are in place to deal with such important matters.

Are there weaknesses even in such a special committee of top management? One has to recognize that where the complaint is against a deliberate policy of top management itself—such as Ford President Lee Iaccoca's determination that the Pinto's price could not be over $2,000 and that all engineering decisions had to stay within that ceiling —a Good Practices committee might simply ratify top management's own policies. But the awareness by management that a review committee has been officially informed of an alleged unsafe product or process, and the possibility that this review could be used in any future lawsuit or government regulatory action as proof that management has been put on notice of a problem, cannot help but lead to a more serious examination of issues and alternatives than where there is no such mechanism in operation.

For whistle-blowing issues that involve clearly illegal practices, another possible mechanism is the creation of a company inspector-general system. In 1978, when I conducted a seminar in New York City on employee rights issues for a group of about a hundred American Telephone and Telegraph Company managers, the newspapers were filled with lurid stories alleging that top executives of two state Bell Telephone companies arranged payoffs to state regulatory officials and demanded sexual relations from female employees. Since these were clear violations of AT&T policies, a member of the AT&T Legal Department expressed surprise that no employees in those two companies used the available remedy. "The office of the Legal Department in New York City was always open to them." The skeptical laughter that greeted this comment expressed the sense of most AT&T executives in the room that this distant mechanism wasn't seen as a real alternative to employees whose top executives were giving the orders.

This suggests that where positive wrongdoing is involved and not matters of judgment about safety or health, companies might do well to take a leaf from the Army and the recent successful practice in the federal executive branch.[10] The appointment of an Inspector General, the creation of a "hot-line" procedure to report illegal conduct, and regular appearances of the Inspector General at local plants and offices to talk confidentially with employees could work quite well in these kinds of whistle-blowing cases. Fraudulent accounting, illegal campaign contributions, false reporting to government contracting agencies, acceptance of bribes from contractors, and similar types of improper conduct would seem tailor-made for investigation and action by an Inspector General within the corporation. Having the report of the Inspector General regularly reviewed by the Board of Directors would add to the effectiveness of this procedure.

Some companies today have Audit Committees as a part of their Board of Directors, and it might be assumed that this fulfills the Inspector General function. But an audit committee usually holds a major investigation of company practices in response to public accusations by stockholders, government officials, or the media. Since an individual employee might have difficulty in getting to the Audit Committee, an Inspector General would still seem to be a necessary instrument in whistle-blowing cases, especially if that official has the authority to put an issue to the Audit Committee when that seemed desirable.

Still another aspect of the internal remedies involves the effect on whistle-blowing problems of the employee-participation and work-reorganization programs that quite a few American companies are currently using to improve employee satisfaction and the quality of work life. These usually involve various kinds of work-committee, plant meetings, or other "team" approaches to making decisions that were once "top down" management directives.

At a 1978 meeting in Washington sponsored by the Public Affairs Council, one corporate executive listening to an account of whistle-blowing cases commented, "That couldn't happen in our company. We have a participative-management system that encourages people to speak up when they feel anything wrong is taking place. The issue would be aired fully in a way that wouldn't cover up anything or automatically ratify what management had done."[11] This comment suggests that those companies that are using employee-participation approaches—from project teams and annual employee town meetings to total-plant participative mechanisms—provide an atmosphere for raising problems that is more hospitable to resolving whistle-blowing charges than the hierarchical management tradition.

My judgment is that this can be a major aid as long as one does not see a participative environment as a complete solution to whistle-blowing issues. That is, no matter how many committees, teams, and other cooperative mechanisms a company has, someone has to make a decision at a given level of authority, and that decision—if unacceptable to the complaining employee—has to be carried to the next level upward. Finally, some authority—and it will usually be top management alone in the nonunion setting—will have to make the final company decision. A participative environment promises to resolve many initial whistle-blowing issues successfully, but other conflict-resolution mechanisms will still be required when an employee will not accept the decision reached at intermediate levels.

For companies that have scientific, technical, and professional employees working for them, and recognizing the growing problems of risk-assessment involved in product safety, employee safety, and environmental protection, managements might consider developing a special procedure along the lines installed in mid-1980 by the U.S. Nuclear Regulatory Commission.[12] The NRC policy grows out of the First Amendment free speech rights of government employees, their right to communicate with Congress, and the whistle-blower protections of the 1978 Civil Service Reform Act, so that it unfolds in a very different legal and organizational climate than private employment. However, its philosophy and procedures are worth consideration in the corporate world.

The NRC defines a "differing professional opinion" as "a conscientious expression of professional judgment on any matter relating to NRC's mission or organizational activities. . . ." To handle those differing opinions that cannot be resolved through normal discussions with co-workers and supervisors, or by the agency's Open Door system, the employee submits a written statement to NRC management outlining the existing policy or practice, the employee's disagreement and the basis for it, the consequences that could arise if the policy is not changed, and any previous reviews or reconsiderations of the policy that the employee is aware of. From that point on, a written record is created, a hearing process is provided, and an appropriate management executive either accepts the recommended change or decides it is not persuasive.

The NRC's Office of Management and Program Analysis provides the Commission with quarterly reports of all such differing professional opinions filed and their outcomes, and these are also filed in the public document room so that experts, the public, and the media can learn of them. The NRC expressly forbids retaliation against an employee for filing a differing professional opinion, spelling out all the informal means of harassment as well as direct retaliation that are not to be used. Each year, a Special Review Panel of NRC employees and outsiders will go over the handling of differing professional opinions not only to see that the system is working properly but also to suggest merit awards for employees whose differing professional opinions "made significant contributions to the agency or to public safety. . . ."

All of these internal complaint and appeal mechanisms offer important procedures to institutionalize the enforcement of the company's principles and policies. But what if management does not adopt such standards, or issues boilerplate statements that it does not follow? What external mechanisms should American society install in those situations?

Before discussing these remedies, it is important to note that almost all the writing on whistle blowing—by courts, arbitrators, business executives, public-interest group leaders, and civil liberties advocates— stresses that employees have a general obligation to raise their protest inside the company before taking it to government bodies or the public. This is to ensure that management has a chance to correct any mistakes that may be the result of inadvertence, bad judgment by subordinates, or a failure to recognize that a problem existed. Since the large corporation is a many-chambered entity, with top management not always aware of what subordinates are doing, and because public denunciation of the company by an employee can cause injury to the corporation's reputation and sales, it is not an unreasonable requirement for the courts, arbitrators, and administrative agencies to say that using the internal procedures is necessary if an employee seeks protection from retaliatory discharge.

This concept was expressed well by Aryeh Neier, formerly executive director of the American Civil Liberties Union, at a panel on "Loyalty and Dissent by Corporate Employees" at the Second National Seminar on Individual Rights in the Corporation.[13] Neier commented that "when an employee seeks to divulge that something wrong is going on to the outside world, or to some specialized government agency, the company has an appropriate claim on the employee that he first speak up inside the company." He then explained that "this duty of loyalty means that the company should be given the right to know first whether the employee believes that management is engaged in something illegal, unethical, or dangerous, and that the employee feels something should be done about it." The company must have "an appropriate internal mechanism for considering such complaints by employees, and a guarantee to employees that they will not suffer any adverse consequences if they make use of that procedure." Where such mechanisms are present, "the loyalty an employee owes the company is to exhaust the remedies that are reasonably provided within the company before going outside," including "a reasonable opportunity for the company to bring its practices into line. . . ."

Neier also cited a positive advantage to management in providing a meaningful internal appeals systems. "The company would get notice that an employee might be going to the outside world. If the company believes that the employee is off his rocker, that the employee is simply talking nonsense, in the process of allowing the employee to go through the internal processes of making the complaint, the company would have an opportunity to ready its case. It could use free speech itself to counter the employee's claim, saying to the outside world, we have this procedure, we've considered this employee's complaints, here are the reasons why this employee's complaints were rejected internally, and why we believe the outside world should reject this criticism as unfounded."

Yet, even this prudent rule ought not to be an ironclad requirement. The company may not have an accessible complaint procedure, or those running the complaint and appeal system may be part of an illegal operation. The employee may have good reason to believe that using the company procedure would unreasonably delay action to protect public safety. The company may have a history of taking reprisals against any employee who complains about such conditions or policies. Or, surfacing a complaint could lead to the destruction of evidence needed for public prosecution. If these conditions are present, the employee is justified in going public, and ought to be able to prove such conditions in any later legal proceeding that may arise, as justification for bypassing the internal machinery. Outside review bodies ought to examine such allegations carefully, to be sure that the internal pipeline was really clogged; but if it was, the employee's resort to direct outside action should be protected as the only effective alternative available.

## External Protections: Existing Laws and New Legal Possibilities

Turning to the external scene, several developments promise to affect the general climate within which corporate employees confront the choice of whether to blow or swallow the whistle. There has been a significant rise in the last few years in criminal prosecutions by both the state and federal governments of corporate officials who engage in false reporting to regulatory agencies. This includes areas such as drug testing, environmental standards, foreign bribery, and product safety. For example, the Olin Corporation, the manager of its Niagara Falls plant, its production manager, and a company chemist were found guilty in August 1979 of filing false reports to the federal government on the amount of mercury dumped by the company into the Niagara River between 1975 and 1977.[14] Earlier in 1979, the Biometrics Testing Company and five of its executives were indicted in federal court for falsifying test results and making false reports to the U.S. Food and Drug Administration; this followed a guilty plea by the company's director of animal testing that he cooperated with the company executives in the false reporting.[15]

In a parallel development, state and federal authorities have been bringing large damage suits against companies for violation of antipollution laws, citing as proof that there was knowing violation of the law the internal memoranda of professional employees and executives who warned that company policies were illegal. One example is the $45 million lawsuit filed by federal and California agencies against Occidental Chemical Company for illegally dumping hazardous material that leaked into underground water supplies near Stockton, California.[16] Another instance is the $124.5 million suit filed by the federal government in December of 1979 against Hooker Chemicals and Plastics Company for dumping chemical wastes in the Love Canal area of upstate New York.[17]

Still further pressure against swallowing the whistle would be applied if Congress were to pass a bill recently introduced by Representative George Miller (Democrat, California) and 55 co-sponsors.[18] If enacted, the proposed law would make it a criminal offense for company officials to fail to inform employees of workplace health hazards discovered by the company. The Miller bill grew out of congressional hearings into the conduct of the asbestos industry (discussed in the Introduction) in suppressing test findings about the dangers of asbestos.

The importance of these trends in criminal prosecutions and damage suits is that professional and executive employees of corporations are becoming aware that cooperating with management violations of law may now lead to their own criminal indictment. This should not only stiffen the resolve of some troubled employees to refuse to cooperate with illegality but should also serve as an incentive to top management to look more carefully into employee warnings that the company's middle-level or senior executives are engaged in illegal activity. An object lesson in 1980 was the sharp criticism in Congress and the media of former Textron chairman G. William Miller for testifying that he "did now know" about foreign bribes made by Textron executives, which led to demands for his resignation as Secretary of the Treasury.[19]

In terms of the individual who does blow the whistle, what are the legal remedies currently available to employees who do not get satisfaction within the company or are fired for their protests? As we already noted, the two most important avenues are antireprisal guarantees in employee-protection or public-protection laws, and private lawsuits for damages on the ground that a discharge violated public policy.

We have included after this chapter a list of major federal laws that contain antireprisal protections. Increasingly, the government agencies charged with enforcing these laws have been publicizing the complaint procedures available to employees under these statutes. To take OSHA as an example, the Department of Labor now distributes a large red and blue poster for display at workplaces. Under a banner head that announces "You Can't Be Punished for Insisting on Job Safety and Health. That's the Law," the poster goes on to spell out how employees can contact OSHA to report any reprisal taken against them, and initiate an "Eleven-C" proceeding. The Department of Labor also distributes a small booklet called "OSHA: Your Workplace Rights in Action" that contains a complete account of "Eleven-C rights" and how to assert them.[20] Many labor unions and other groups distribute this leaflet to their members.

The number of 11-C complaints that OSHA receives has been rising steadily: 752 in 1974; 2,175 in 1976; and 3,100 in 1979.[21] A study of the complaints filed in 1977 showed that 25% of the employees said reprisals were taken against them after they complained to management; 24.6% after they filed a complaint with OSHA; and 21.2% after they refused to continue working on an unsafe site. The remaining grounds included testifying in a proceeding, participating in a safety or health committee, filing a complaint with another government agency, and other grounds.[22]

In early 1979, an OSHA official reported that 16 antireprisal cases had been litigated to that date, with the Robert Elliot case in this book representing one of their "best wins."[23] Voluntary settlements were obtained in 270 cases. But the heavy backload of pending cases remains a cause of concern and has just led the Labor Departent to install a computerized system for managing the more than 3,000 currently pending cases; the goal is to divide these complaints more expeditiously into investigation, negotiation, or litigation. However, the OSHA officials I spoke to felt that the growing number of dangerous substances being identified in workplaces and the potentially harmful effects on workers that are being discovered would probably keep Eleven-C enforcement at high levels in the near future.

While agency protection of whistle blowers under antireprisal guarantees is important, some current limitations in its operations need to be noted. Many cases before the EEOC, OSHA, and other agencies take between one and three years to be processed, due to the shortage of investigators and hearing examiners. While this is partly a matter of budget, it also grows out of agency feelings that it is generally more important to handle substantive issues of race or sex discrimination, workplace dangers, etc., and to remedy the underlying cause than to spend precious resources on the reprisal question alone. This means that many employees and executives face long periods of waiting during which they may be fired from their jobs, cannot get good employment references, and have no legal determination of the validity of their complaint to offer to potential employers. The basic remedy for this problem would seem to be strong presentations by agency leaders before legislative appropriation committees stressing the need for added resources to handle antireprisal cases more speedily; if necessary, the key legislative committees should indicate to agency executives that the legislators regard processing antireprisal complaints not only as a major priority for bringing recalcitrant managements into greater compliance with the rules but also as a vital way of encouraging employees to speak up about illegality. In addition, as state and federal legislatures enact new public-protection laws covering specific industries or general corporate practices, it will be important for legislators to see that antireprisal provisions and procedures for enforcing them are included.

For those employees whose complaints about corporate illegality or impropriety do not fall within the scope of employee protection and public protection laws—and this is often the case today—the other current legal avenue is to bring a lawsuit for damages alleging wrongful discharge. As we noted in the Introduction, the great majority of states still accept the common-law rule that employers can fire an employee at will, unless there is an express contract for a definite period of time, a collective bargaining agreement with a union that requires "just cause" for dismissal, or legislation forbidding termination for a particular reason (such as race discrimination). Where these exceptions are not present, the courts in about 40 states will not look into the reasons for discharge or its reasonableness.

Even when employees bring their cases into the federal courts, by suing their corporation as a legal citizen of another state, the federal courts in such contract cases do not formulate their own rule of law but apply the legal rule of the state found to have been the primary place of employment; this means that most federal courts today also follow the fire-at-will doctrine. As of 1980, therefore, only whistle-blowing employees in about a dozen states (such as Pennsylvania, New Jersey, West Virginia, California, Oregon, and Michigan) can bring damage suits with any confidence that the judges will be willing to look into the facts of the discharge to see whether it violated public policy.

### Three Major Proposals for New Legal Protection

Given this weakness in the legal protection of conscientious whistle blowers, three proposals have been made to change the current state of the law: to enact federal or state legislation to protect whistle blowers in private industry; to pass more general legislation forbidding private employers to engage in "unjust dismissals," with one type being discharge of whistle blowers; and to have state courts change the common-law rule supporting employer prerogative to an approach that allows such courts to examine the propriety of contested discharges.

The first proposal, federal or state legislation to protect whistle blowers, raises several key choices: how to define protected conduct; what body to conduct proceedings on complaints; and what remedies for employees or sanctions for employers to apply. Among the various alternatives, my own preference would be to have a statute that would make it an unfair employment practice for an employer to discharge or take punitive action against any employee who reported to management, or to an outside government agency, conduct by the company that the employee reasonably believed to be illegal, against public policy, or in violation of the company's own rules and procedures. The initial complaint by an employee would go to an independent executive agency, such as the National Labor Relations Board or its state counter-parts, with review by the courts available as it is today for alleged violations of national or state labor-management laws.

The agency would be empowered to conduct a preliminary investi-gation, and either dismiss the complaint or set it for a full hearing before the agency's board. Any hearing would examine whether the employee made use of the available complaint and appeal mechanism provided by the company, or, if not, whether any special circumstances justified such action. It would also examine whether the employee exercised the right of protest in a manner and time that substantially disrupted the conduct of the business; such behavior would be weighed against the way that management responded to the employee's allegation of illegal, danger-ous, or unethical conduct, in order to judge the entire context. Because of the weakness of current remedies—awarding damages to the em-ployee is often quite an acceptable price for large corporations to bear to "get rid of troublemakers," and a damage award still may not enable an employee to get another job in the industry—the board would have two levels of remedies. If it found that the employer acted improperly but in good faith, it could award actual damages, including lawyers' fees, while not requiring the company to rehire the employee. But if it found that the management had acted knowingly and willfully to con-tinue illegal actions, even after the employee pointed them out, then the board could order the employee reinstated and/or assess punitive dam-ages against the company.

The second approach involves the enactment of a federal or state law forbidding "unjust dismissals," with whistle blowing as one form of conduct that the statute would define as unjust. Some experts have advocated adopting "just cause" as the standard, paralleling the rule used in collective bargaining contracts.[24] The difference is that a "just cause" standard puts the burden on the employer to show that dismissal was justified, while "unjust dismissal" requires the employee to estab-lish as a preliminary that a standard of "justness" set by the statute seemed to have been violated; thereafter, the employer would have to prove a proper basis for the action. Because of the greater variety of subjective factors as to employee performance and effectiveness in-volved in professional, sales, and executive ranks compared to assembly line and white-collar office jobs, I think the "unjust dismissal" standard is preferable in the nonunion context. The British use such an "unjust dismissal" standard in their labor law, and they have been quite success-ful over the past decade in terms of screening out frivolous complaints, conducting fair hearings, and reaching balanced judgments.[25]

The third approach would be to convince a majority of state courts to change the common-law rule. A steady stream of law review commentary during the past 20 years has called on the courts to abandon the employment-at-will concept as inappropriate for contemporary society.[26] These authors point out the disproportionate power between large employers and employees and the fact that unions do not cover three-fourths of the workforce; the punitive, "blacklist" effect of dismissals on employees, especially those with specialities in a given skill or industry; and the growing stake that society itself has in protecting conscientious whistle blowers from punitive action and thereby bringing corporate actions closer into line with legal rules.

Some legal experts have urged the courts to examine the propriety of contested discharges only when there is legislation present that expresses public policy on the matter involved in the employee's claim. For example, a federal court of appeals ruled in December of 1979 that it was the presence of a Pennsylvania law forbidding employers to make the taking of a polygraph ("lie-detector") test a condition of employment or continuation of employment that allowed the court to look into the factual merits of an employee's claim that he was fired by Firestone Tire and Rubber Company because he refused to take such a test.[27] Other experts, and some state courts, believe that the judiciary should be able to look at the grounds of a discharge and decide, even in the absence of legislation, whether the court believes public policy has been violated by the employer's action.[28] Examples are court rulings awarding damages to employees fired for going on jury duty,[29] for refusing to falsify medical records,[30] for refusing to give false testimony in a legal proceeding,[31] or for filing legitimate workmen's compensation claims (in states that do not forbid such employer conduct by statute).[32] While this debate over the judicial standard reflects a broader debate in our society over the degree of independent intervention courts should exercise in relation to legislative actions, my own view is that the great variety of employment settings and whistle-blowing situations makes it very difficult to imagine 50 states specifying by legislation every context of improper dismissal. Therefore, I would favor a common-law rule that allows the courts to apply legislative declarations of public policy but not to be limited to those situations, and to have the power to apply general public policy considerations.

How would each or all of these three new legal protections for whistle blowers be likely to affect the institutional and social considerations raised earlier in this chapter? Clearly, there would be an increase in legal contests and in the time and money that companies would have to spend in defending their personnel actions to "outsiders." And, there is no doubt that agencies and courts would be examining many company policies that today are not reviewed. But that is what society expects to happen when it feels that threats to public health, safety, and welfare make it necessary to define new legal duties, give persons rights, and create remedies to vindicate such rights. The meaningful question is whether there would be such an avalanche of litigation that society ought not to embark on this course of action.

Although no one can predict scientifically the way new legal measures would be administered, we can look at several related legal systems to gauge what is likely to occur. First of all, arbitrators, agencies, and courts have proved quite adept and tough-minded in weighing employee allegations about management illegalities against the company explanations, and in examining whether employees used the machinery and proper techniques for complaint before making charges public. In fact, of eight recent arbitrator cases involving just such issues, under "just cause" standards of collective bargaining, seven were decided *against* the employees and for the companies.[33] And, while there are changing tides in the supposedly "pro-company" or "pro-employee" perspective of various state and federal regulatory agencies, the long-term trend is for a body of principles and standards to be developed that reflects society's sense of the right balance, and legislators know how to intervene to bring such an acceptable balance into operation where it may become distorted.

So far, the discussion of external legal remedies has focused on the types of situations in which whistle blowers allege that clearly illegal or potentially illegal conduct is taking place. The third situation—disputed business policies—also deserves attention. Essentially, since the company's policies are by definition not illegal, the basic issue is one of employee free speech. When may employees publicly criticize the product, business services, investments, or social policies of their employer and claim the protection of free speech privileges?

A current case may help to sharpen the analysis. On July 21, 1979, seven black employees of the Zellerbach Paper Company in Los Angeles wrote a letter to the Los Angeles Board of Education protesting the Board's making an award to the company's personnel director for affirmative action progress by Zellerbach. The employees asked the Board to explain why it had "failed to look at Zellerbach's total affirmative action picture." They expressed "shock" and "dismay" to learn that the personnel director, who they said was "the standard bearer of the bigoted position of racism at Zellerbach Paper Company," was to be honored by a public agency. They also noted that the local federal Equal Employment Opportunity office had recently filed a lawsuit charging Zellerbach with violation of antidiscrimination and affirmative action duties.

On August 3, without any preliminary warning or hearing, the seven employees were dismissed and told to be off the plant grounds within 15 minutes. In its letter of termination, the company told the employees: "Your action of disloyal conduct which could affect the relationship with a valued customer will not be tolerated by the company." Calling the charges of racism "unfounded defamatory statements," the company told the discharged employees they had "no right or privilege whatever to injure the company and its employees by jeopardizing its reputation and relationships with its customers."

The seven employees turned to the American Civil Liberties Union of Southern California, which is now suing to obtain their reinstatement. The ACLU also called on the Board of Education to investigate the company's "repression" of First Amendment rights of free speech by its employees, "who are also taxpayers and citizens of Los Angeles County." To this, a vice president and manager of Zellerbach's regional operations replied, "We recognize the right of all our employees to seek redress of grievances by all appropriate means. But this goes beyond that."[34]

The Zellerbach case poses sharply the question of where to draw the line between rights as a citizen and rights as an employee. There is little doubt that these employees would have been legally protected had they just filed an EEO compliant with a state or federal agency, and probably if they had publicized the substance of that complaint to the press or community groups. And, if they had been spokesmen for a union and had criticized Zellerbach's racial policies as part of an organizing drive or in a collective bargaining situation, they would also have been legally protected from reprisal. But the courts have generally held that individual employees do not enjoy the same right of protected criticism as union leaders.[35] And, even where there are collective bargaining contracts, many of these include a clause requiring individual employees to refrain from disloyal acts that would harm the company's business or public reputation.[36] Although we have certainly left the era when arbitrators or courts would interpret such loyalty clauses as requiring Ford workers not to drive General Motors cars to the company parking lot, how should the line between loyalty and protected dissent be defined?

The American Civil Liberties Union recently adopted the following policy on employee free speech in the corporate world:[37]

> In all cases, the employee's right to free speech and association should be limited only by minimal and traditionally acceptable time, place and manner regulations, provided that the employee's exercise of the right does not substantially, materially and directly interfere with his or her bona fide job performance, or substantially, materially and directly obstruct other employees. This should not protect speech which directly interferes with the ability of the employee adequately to perform his/her job.

In the debate leading up to the adoption of this broad free speech doctrine, the ACLU rejected additional qualifications that would have allowed the balancing of free speech rights against organizational interests such as efficient performance or customer/public reputation, or exceptions for false charges and malicious speech. The ACLU's view is that the courts are all too quick to limit free speech by considering such organizational values, and a balancing approach ought not to be the ACLU's standard.

My sense is that the courts both will and ought to extend to the private sector the same basic rules for individual private employees that are applied to government employee free speech. The time, place, and manner of expression can be constrained, and conduct that directly obstructs work could be held unprotected. But I also think that direct attempts to interfere with the business of the employer, by making attacks on the company to its customers or by organizing the organization of boycotts of its products, is conduct that is citizen protected but not necessarily employee protected. Drawing the line between pure expression and conduct that is more than speech would have to be done by the courts on a factual basis, and might depend somewhat on the type of issue involved.

Summing up the external legal remedies, I think that we need to strengthen the antireprisal machinery under employee protection and public protection statutes; keep the pressure for lawful behavior on corporate officials by prosecuting those who file false reports to the government and recovering damages against companies that ignore employee warnings of illegal conduct; create a general statutory protection for private whistle blowers through federal or state legislation, carried out by executive agency proceedings; persuade the courts to create a new and more realistic common-law rule as to employee rights against unjust dismissal; and apply First Amendment–based protections to assure employee free speech.

## Private Support for Whistle Blowers

Finally, the lonely, painful, and financially destructive experiences of most whistle blowers, including those of the ten persons whose stories are told in this book, cry out for the creation of supporting mechanisms from the private sector. For unionized employees, the support of the local and international union can be a major factor; there are positive signs that many unions have become increasingly concerned about whistle-blowing issues involving workplace safety, worker health, intrusive employee surveillance, dangers to customers and communities, and related topics.[38] Professional societies in fields such as engineering, chemistry, computer science, law, auditing, and several others have begun to pay greater attention to the ethical dilemmas and responsibilities of their members working in industry (and government); several recent conferences and projects have been organized to develop new ethical codes, better machinery for professional societies to investigate charges of unethical demands, and procedures for applying sanctions against employers who fire professionals for refusing to accept unethical orders.[39] The Society for Ethical Culture organized a national project to assist whistle blowers who have "put their careers on the line" by exposing illegal or unethical practices by employers.[40] And, many consumer groups, environmental defense groups, civil liberties organizations, and other public interest groups have become active in supporting whistle blowers who need legal counsel or other assistance to press their cases.[41] Given the resources in money, talent, and influence that the business community possesses, such assistance represents the kind of effort to assure fair play and a fair hearing that American society has long supported. This private action is needed partly to obtain justice for the individual employee who conscientiously blows the whistle on corporate misconduct. It is also needed to help campaign for the new organizational policies and legal machinery that can transform the present unequal contest between some corporate managements and whistle blowers into a system that better serves the interests of our whole society.

## Some Guides for Potential Whistle Blowers

The personal accounts in this book can be read in part as cautionary tales and how-to-do-it stories for potential whistle blowers in industry.

They suggest to me the following steps that any potential whistle-blowing employee ought to have in mind in considering a move from ethical concern to corrective action.

1. Be very analytic and careful in assessing the facts on which your protest would be based. Can you document company wrongdoing in a way that would persuade a skeptical reporter or a dispassionate judge that the actions and motives of management are what you say they are? If you were to put yourself into the position of the chairman of the board of that company acting ethically to advance both the firm's well-being and the public interest, would you follow the course of conduct that your protest as an employee calls for? Are you sure you know all the facts and the relevant law that are known to management about this situation? Is it possible that personality conflicts, career disappoint-ments, or plain ego gratification might be affecting your judgment in this case? And, if all the answers to these questions lead you to believe you are right, are you prepared to take on the grueling and lengthy personal trial that becoming a whistle blower will surely mean to you, your family, and your friends?

2. If you decide to go ahead, determine just what kind of company conduct you are protesting. If it is clear illegality or potentially illegal or unsafe conduct, you can hope to be vindicated by internal or external appeals and perhaps still work at this job or in the same industry. But if it is lawful business or social policies of the company that you feel you must protest, be aware that you will probably have to give up your job in order to make your witness. You will be choosing the role of a policy critic rather than that of the loyal employee declining to do illegal or dangerous things. As a government employee, you might be pro-tected as a matter of free speech rights; but in private industry, the law does not provide employees with the right to be a public critic of lawful policies in ways that harm a company's name or business. You may still feel that protesting a policy that you feel is unjust or unethical is something you must do. But if that is the case, you should recognize that you are staking your prospects of continuing to work in that firm or industry on the outcome of an appeal to public vindication, and a publicly compelled change in the outlook of corporate managers.

3. Inform yourself fully of the procedures in your company for appealing the policy that concerns you up through the chain of com-mand to the highest available levels of management. Get a written copy of such complaint and appeal procedures, and follow them rigorously,

unless your situation is one of the special cases already discussed in this chapter, where formal complaint would lead to destruction of evidence or other coverups.

4. Before and while moving through the internal channels, document your position at every step of the way with records, letters, and other hard evidence, including taping or stenographic reporting of hearings or meetings whenever that is possible. While there are ethical and even legal questions raised by such accumulation of evidence by an employee, the failure to gather such evidence has been fatal to many a whistle blower's later appeals to outside agencies or the courts.

5. When moving into either internal or external channels of complaint and appeal, seriously consider getting an attorney, or contacting a public interest group, professional society, labor union, or other organization active in your area of concern or industry. The judgment and advice of such sympathetic but less personally involved persons is usually vital to wise choices of action and strategy in each whistle-blowing case. And, such help will be a vital resource if the issue becomes a cause célèbre.

6. If the problem is one that is regulated by law, such as an occupational safety, discrimination, product-safety, or environmental-protection situation, learn what the requirements and procedures are for lodging a complaint with the relevant government agency. Be very sure to find out what the law may set as the time limits within which reports of alleged violations must be reported, and whether complaints must be made first to the company officials before being lodged with the regulatory agency. This may raise complicated issues of when to turn to government agencies and when to stay within the company. But not to know what the rules are in this matter is to risk being barred later from invoking the antireprisal guarantees of the law for failing to report the matter in the time and manner required.

7. If you are fired or forced to resign because of your protest, be aware that your right to discuss the case in public is strong but not unlimited. In an important 1979 case in New York, a former employee of KLM Royal Dutch Airlines alleged publicly that he was forced out of the company for protesting illegal kickbacks and other improper payments; he gave extensive interviews to the press supporting his charges and produced internal company documents. KLM obtained an injunction in the New York court forbidding the employee to discuss the details of the case, on the ground that this would reveal trade secrets

and other proprietary information of great value to the company's competitors. Fortunately, this gag ruling was reversed on appeal, in an opinion that held such a sweeping injunction to violate the ex-employee's First Amendment rights.[42] On the whole therefore, whistle blowers can discuss their cases publicly under free speech rights, even though there could be some limitations while litigation is pending or if truly confidential proprietary information were involved.

8. If you cannot win damages or reinstatement through an appeal to a government regulatory agency with jurisdiction over the issue you have raised, be ready to consider a lawsuit alleging that your discharge or punitive treatment violates public policy. While most states, as we have discussed, do not presently accept such a suit for wrongful discharge in private employment, the tide of judicial opinion is shifting, and if you can afford the financial and other costs involved, you might not only win your case but also help to move another state into the camp that recognizes such a cause of action.

Even if all these cautions and prudential suggestions are followed, there is no guarantee that an employee will either be right in what he or she alleges to be true or that the industrial version of capital punishment will not be applied and prevail. But good strategy never hurt a good cause, and in the balance of resources between employee and corporation, the employee needs and can profit from every bit of help.

## Prospects for the Future

The ten stories in this collection highlight the fact that, as this concluding chapter has argued, we are entering a new and turbulent period in the relationship between employees and managers in the United States. The old order of corporate autonomy and legal immunity that marked the pre-1960 era is clearly dead. The transition period of 1960–1980 has closed with some important but still undigested changes in the legal rules and public conceptions relating to corporate management. What American society, public policy makers, and company managers will make of these new conditions is what remains to be determined in the next period.

What seems clear is that powerful forces for significant institutional and legal reform are firmly in place and will grow stronger. Many employees are now going to work with new commitments about their personal responsibilities, obligations to public safety and welfare, and rights of expression on the job; they will not be as easily silenced or co-opted as earlier generations of corporate employees. An already large and steadily growing latticework of law and government regulations to protect employees and the public has been enacted and is waiting to be applied by administrative agencies to new whistle-blowing situations. In the courts, the common-law rule of employment-at-will is under sharp attack; the signs are unmistakable that this doctrine will not long withstand the growing assaults by legal experts on its relevance or justice for the employment realities of the late 20th century. Whether by statute or judicial rule, we will soon have a basic law forbidding "unjust dismissal," as do almost all the other industrialized democracies. Within the corporation, there is deep ferment among personnel and human resources managers leading toward the adoption of new approaches to work organization, project and plant decision-making, and other aspects of what has come to be called the quality-of-work-life issue, involving new modes of employee participation that encourage greater expression. There will also be increasing activity by labor, consumer, environmental, minority, civil liberty, and religious groups in the 1980s in support of whistle blowers individually and also calling for general adoption of new mechanisms of internal and external protection for conscientious dissent.

Finally, while few corporate managements are happy with the heavy burden of employee litigation that existing employee protection laws have precipitated, or the elaborate administrative and financial costs created by public-protection laws, I find a growing sense among leading companies that these laws are essentially just and necessary. Therefore, the task for management and society in the 1980s and 1990s is to find creative ways to apply them that will minimize burdensome litigation and regulation, assess risks and costs in a sensitive way that balances enterprise needs as well as the public interest, and harness the creative energies and imagination of the 80 million people on whose talents and commitment the productivity of the private sector ultimately depends.

This represents a challenge to American society as a whole and to its business institutions. How well we respond to its moral as well as practical imperatives will help determine not only the quality of working life in American industry during the next decades but also the integrity and justice of our social order.

## NOTES

1. John Z. De Lorean with J. Patrick Wright, *On A Clear Day You Can See General Motors* (Caroline House, 1979), Chapter Four, "Why Moral Men Make Immoral Decisions."

2. To be published in *Proceedings of the National Seminars on Individual Rights in the Corporation, 1978, 1979, 1980.*

3. Interview by Alan F. Westin with executive of chemical company, 1978.

4. For overviews of these mechanisms in the corporate world, see *Policies for Unorganized Employees,* Personnel Policies Forum Survey No. 125, Bureau of National Affairs, April 1979, and *Nonunion Complaint Systems: A Corporate Appraisal,* Report No. 770, The Conference Board, 1980.

5. For a description of IBM's policy, see "IBM's Guidelines to Employee Privacy: An Interview with Frank T. Cary," *Harvard Business Review,* Volume 54, Number 5, September–October 1976, pp. 82–90.

6. These companies made presentations on their Ombudsman programs at the First and Second National Seminars on Individual Rights in the Corporation, in 1978 and 1979. They are to be published in a casebook on employee rights programs to be issued by McGraw-Hill in 1981.

7. Materials provided by Citibank, N.A., February 1980; official promulgation by Citibank was to take place later in 1980.

8. *Edwards v. Citibank,* 418 N.Y.S. 2d 269 (1979), dismissing the complaint under the employment-at-will doctrine.

9. Statement to Alan F. Westin by Citibank personnel executive, December, 1979.

10. "GAO Says Tips Over 'Hot Line' Are Curbing Government Fraud," New York *Times,* December 10, 1979, p. A24.

11. This took place during a forum on employee rights issues at the Public Affairs Council in December, 1978, Washington, D.C., at which Alan F. Westin was one of the three speakers.

12. "Proposed Policy and Procedures for Differing Professional Opinions," NUREG-0567," 1979. This was about to be promulgated early in 1980 after completion of a period for public comments in the latter part of 1979.

13. To be published in *Proceedings . . . , supra* note 2.

14. "Olin Company and 3 Former Aides Guilty in a Mercury-Dumping Case," New York *Times,* August 19, 1979, p. B2.

15. Henry Goldman, "Lab Chief Admits Faking Tests," The *Record* (New Jersey), July 15, 1979, p. A14.

16. Wallace Turner, "Chemical Company in California Sued in Ground-Water Pollution," New York *Times,* December 19, 1979, p. B3.

17. Irvin Molotsky, "Hooker Co. Sued By Justice Department Over Love Canal," New York *Times,* December 21, 1979, p. B2.

18. H. R. 4793 (House of Representatives, 96th Cong., 2d Sess., 1980).

19. "Treasury Secretary Accused," *Time,* February 11, 1980, p. 31.

20. "OSHA: Your Workplace Rights in Action," OSHA 3032, Office of Information, 1978.

21. Letter to Alan F. Westin, from Thomas Buckley, OSHA, October 18, 1979.

22. "FY 1977 Completed Cases Survey," OSHA, March 24, 1978.

23. Information furnished by Thomas Buckley, OSHA, October, 1979.

24. See, for example, Alfred W. Blumrosen, "Strangers No More: All Workers Are Entitled to 'Just Cause' Protection under Title VII," *Industrial Relations Law Journal,* Vol. 2, 519–566 (1978); Cornelius J. Peck, "Unjust Discharges From Employment: A Necessary Change in the Law," *Ohio State Law Journal,* Vol. 40, No. 1, 1979, 1–49.

25. Dudley Jackson, *Unfair Dismissal: How and Why the Law Works* (Cambridge: Cambridge University Press, 1976).

26. In addition to the articles cited in note 24, see: Lawrence E. Blades, Employment at Will vs. Individual Freedom: On Limiting the Abusive Exercise of Employer Power," *Columbia Law Review,* Vol. 67 (1967), 1404–1435; Clyde W. Summers, "Individual Protection against Unjust Dismissal: Time for a Statute," *Virginia Law Review,* Vol. 62 (1976), 481–532; Phillip I. Blumberg, "Corporate Responsibility and the Employee's Duty of Loyalty and Obedience: A Preliminary Inquiry," *Oklahoma Law Review,* Vol. 24, No. 3 (1971), 279–304; Staughton Lynd, "Employee Speech in the Private and Public Workplace: Two Doctrines or One?," *Industrial Relations Law Journal,* Vol. 1 (1977), 711–754; "Implied Contract Rights to Job Security," *Stanford Law Review,* Vol. 26 (1974), 335–369; "A Remedy for the Discharge of Professional Employees Who Refuse to Perform Unethical or Illegal Acts: A Proposal in Aid of Professional Ethics," *Vanderbilt Law Review,* Vol. 28 (1975), 805–840; "Protecting the Private Sector At-Will Employee Who 'Blows the Whistle': A Cause of Action Based upon Determinants of Public Policy," *Wisconsin Law Review,* 1977, 777–812; Thomas Gelb, "Non-Statutory Causes of Action for an Employer's Termination of an 'At-Will' Employment Relationship: A Possible Solution to the Economic Imbalance in the Employer-Employee Relationship," *N.Y. Law School Law Review,* Vol. 24, No. 3 (1979), 743–769; Robert Coulson, "Rising Expectations for Job Security in Corporate America," *New York Law Journal,* Jan. 10, 1980, p. 1; Mary Ann Glendon and Edward R. Lev, "Changes in the Bonding of the Employment Relationship: An Essay on the New Property," *XX Boston College Law Review* 457–484 (1979).

27. *Parks v. Firestone Tire and Rubber Co.,* No. 79–1561, U.S. Court of Appeals for the Third Circuit, December 31, 1979.

28. See the *Wisconsin Law Review* comment in note 26, and the Peck article in note 24.

29. *Nees v. Hocks,* 536 P. 2d 512 (1975); *Reuther v. Fowler & Williams, Inc.,* 386 A. 2d 119 (1978).

30. *Hinrichs v. Tranquillaire Hospital,* 352 So. 2d 1130 (1977).

31. *Petermann v. International Brotherhood, Etc.,* 344 P. 2d 25 (1959).

32. *Sventko v. The Kroger Co.,* 69 Mich. App. 644 (1976); *Frampton v. Central Indiana Gas Co.,* 297 N.E. 2d 125 (1973).

33. The eight decisions were: Appalachian Power Co., 73-2 *Arb.* P. 8496, Dec. 21, 1973; *Gold Kist, Inc.,* 78-1 *Arb.* P. 8165, Feb. 20, 1977; *Southern Bell Tel. & Tg.,* 77-2 *Arb,* P. 8449, Sept. 19, 1977; *Davenport Good Samaritan Center,* 78-2 *Arb,* P. 8441, Sept. 1, 1978; *Forest City Publishing,* 58 L.A. 773, May 22, 1972; *Thiokol Chemical Corp.,* 52 L.A. 1254, June 21, 1969; *Factory Services Inc.,* 70 L.A. 1088, May 30, 1978; *Northern Indiana Public Services Co.,* 69 L.A. 201, July 19, 1977.

34. Anthony Price, "Zellerbach Fires 7 Workers for Letter to School Board," *Open Forum* (American Civil Liberties Union of Southern California), September 1979, p. 3; Paul Schrade and Miriam Ludwig, "Workers' Rights Group Zeroes in on Defense of Workplace Freedoms," *Ibid.,* December, 1979, p. 4.

35. See, for example, *Anco Insulators,* 1980 CCH NLRB No. 16, 774.

36. See Lawrence Stessin, "Blue-Collar Crime: Chewing Out The Boss," New York *Times,* July 1, 1979, F3.

37. Policy on Free Speech Rights of Corporate Employees, in "Summary of Board Actions Taken at March 3–4 Meeting," American Civil Liberties Union, March 9, 1979.

38. See the testimony of various unions at the hearings on "Pressures in Today's Workplace," *Oversight Hearings before the Subcommittee on Labor-Management Relations,* Committee on Education and Labor, House of Representatives, 96th Cong., 1st Sess., 1979; the support of the Building and Construction Trades Department, AFL-CIO, for the Corporate Democracy Act of 1980; the campaign of the Brotherhood of Locomotive Engineers in support of H.R. 1540, a bill to protect whistle blowers under the Federal Railway Safety Act of 1970; the United Auto Workers' success at getting an employee right to see his/her own personnel record into the national contract with General Motors; the 1980 campaign by the United Steelworkers for greater job safety and employee privacy rights; and many other examples.

39. Professional Ethics Project of the American Association for the Advancement of Science, under grants from the National Science Foundation and National Endowment for the Humanities; "Reports on IEEE's First Ethics Case," *IEEE Technology and Society* No. 22 (1979), p. 1, 8.

40. "You're Blowing the Whistle on Wrongdoing?" leaflet issued by the Ethical Society Whistle Blowing Project, Washington, D.C.

41. The American Civil Liberties Union; the public-interest law firms and action groups in various fields associated with Ralph Nader; the Environmental Defense Fund; women's rights groups such as Working Women United that support attacks on sexual harassment illustrate the organizations available.

42. *KLM Royal Dutch Airlines v. DeWit,* 418 N.Y.S. 2d 63 (1979).

# Selected Bibliography

## BOOKS AND MONOGRAPHS

Baum, Robert J., and Flores, Albert. *Ethical Problems in Engineering.* New York: Center for the Study of the Human Dimensions of Science and Technology, 1978.

Deutsch, Arnold R. *The Human Resources Revolution: Communicate or Litigate.* New York: McGraw-Hill Book Company, 1979.

Ewing, David W. *Freedom Inside the Organization: Bringing Civil Liberties to the Workplace.* New York: E.P. Dutton, 1977.

Farley, Lin. *Sexual Shakedown: The Sexual Harassment of Women on the Job.* New York: McGraw-Hill Book Company, 1978.

Hearings before the Subcommittee on Labor-Management Relations, Committee on Education and Labor, House of Representatives, *Pressures in Today's Workplace.* Washington, D.C.: U.S. Government Printing Office, 1979, Vols. 1 and 2, 1979.

Jackson, Dudley. *Unfair Dismissal: How and Why the Law Works.* Cambridge: Cambridge University Press, 1975.

Lawless, Edward W. *Technology and Social Shock.* New Brunswick: Rutgers University Press, 1977.

Lovins, Amory. *Non-Nuclear Futures: The Case for an Ethical Energy Strategy.* Friends of the Earth, International-SanFrancisco/Ballinger Pub. Co., Cambridge, Mass., 1975.

MacKinnon, Catharine A. *Sexual Harassment of Working Women.* New Haven: Yale University, 1979.

Nader, Ralph, Petkas, Peter J., and Blackwell, Kate (eds.), *Whistle Blowing: The Report of the Conference on Professional Responsibility.* New York: Grossman Publishers, 1972.

Nuclear Regulatory Commission. *Proposed Policy and Procedures for Differing Professional Opinions.* Washington, D.C.: Office of Management and Program Analysis, U.S. Nuclear Regulatory Commission, October 1979.

Parker, Donn. B. *Ethical Conflicts in Computer Science and Technology.* Arlington: AFIPS Press, 1978.

Uris, Auren. *Executive Dissent.* New York: AMACOM, 1978.

Westin, Alan F., and Salisbury, Stephan. *Individual Rights in the Corporation: A Reader on Employee Rights.* New York: Pantheon, 1980.

Whiteside, Thomas. *Computer Capers: Tales of Electronic Thievery, Embezzlement and Fraud.* New York: Thomas Y. Crowell Company, 1978.

## ARTICLES

Note. "Employee Challenges to Arbitral Awards: A Model for Protecting Individual Rights under the Collective Bargaining Agreement." *University of Pennsylvania Law Review,* 125 (June 1977) 1310.

Anon. "When Must A Lawyer Blow The Whistle?" *Business Week,* 21 May 1979, p. 117.

Anon. "Fired Citibank Employee's Suit Dismissed." *American Banker,* 26 June 1979, p. 3.

Anon. "Sexual Harassment Lands Companies in Court." *Business Week,* 1 October 1979, p. 120.

Anon. "GAO Says Tips Over 'Hot Line' Are Curbing Government Fraud." *New York Times,* 10 December 1979, p. A24.

Ashford, Nicholas A., and Katz, Judith I. "Unsafe Working Conditions: Employee Rights Under the Labor Management Relations Act and the Occupational Safety and Health Act." *Notre Dame Lawyer,* 52 (June 1972), 802.

Baker, Donald P. "Proving Sexual Harassment Is A Struggle." *Washington Post,* 24 October 1979, p. A7.

Blades, Lawrence E. "Employment At Will vs. Individual Freedom: On Limiting the Abusive Exercise of Employer Power." *Columbia Law Review,* 67 (1967), 1404.

Blumberg, Philip I. "Corporate Responsibility and the Employee's Duty of Loyalty and Obedience: A Preliminary Inquiry." *Oklahoma Law Review,* 24 (1971), 279.

Blumrosen, Alfred W. "Strangers No More: All Workers Are Entitled To 'Just Cause' Protection Under Title VII." *Industrial Relations Law Journal,* 2 (1978), 519.

Bronson, Gail. "Worker's Right To Know." *Wall Street Journal,* 1 July 1977, p. 1.

Carson, Teresa. "Employee Rights Issues Are On The Rise." *American Banker,* 30 July 1979, p. 1.

Chalk, Rosemary, and von Hippel, Frank. "Due Process for Dissenting 'Whistle-Blowers.' " *Technology Review,* June/July 1979, p. 49.

Conway, John H. "Protecting the Private Sector At-Will Employee Who "Blows the Whistle": A Cause of Action Based Upon the Determinants Of Public Policy." *Wisconsin Law Review* (1977), 777.

Coulson, Robert, "Rising Expectations for Job Security in Corporate America," *New York Law Journal,* Jan. 10, 1980, p. 1.

Ewing, David. "What Business Thinks About Employee Rights." *Harvard Business Review,* September-October 1977, p. 81.

Ewing, David W., and Banks, Pamela M., "Listening and Responding to Employees' Concerns: An Interview with A. W. Clausen [Bank of America]," *Harvard Business Review,* Jan.-Feb. 1980, p. 101.

Gelb, Thomas. "Non-Statutory Causes of Action for an Employer's Termination of an 'At Will' Employment Relationship: A Possible Solution to the Economic Imbalance in the Employer-Employee Relationship." *New York Law Review,* vol. 24, no. 3, 1979, pp. 743–769.

Glenden, Mary Ann, and Lev, Edward R. "Changes in the Bonding of the Employment Relationship: An Essay on the New Property," XX *Boston College Law Review,* 457 (1979).

Greenfield, Meg. "Blowing the Whistle." *Newsweek,* 25 September 1978, p. 112.

Hacker, Andrew. "Loyalty—and the Whistle Blower." *Across the Board,* November 1978, p. 4.

Henner, Sionag. "California's Controls on Employer Abuse of Employee Political Rights." *Stanford Law Review,* 22 (May 1970), 1015.

Hoerr, John. "A Warning That Worker Discontent Is Rising." *Business Week,* 4 June 1979, p. 152.

Holden, Constance. "Rattlesnake Defender to Keep His Job." *Science,* 2 November 1979, p. 541.

Holloway, William J. "Fired Employees Challenging Terminable-At-Will Doctrine." *The National Law Journal,* 19 February 1979, p. 22.

Kennedy, Carol S., M.D. "One Doctor's Fight for Reform." *Medical Dimensions,* May 1978, p. 24.

Krucoff, Carol. "Careers: Sexual Harassment on the Job." *Washington Post,* 25 July 1979, p. B5.

Locklin, Bruce. "Whistleblowing in Maywood." *The Bergen Record,* 2 October 1979, p. B–26.

Lynd, Staughton. "Employee Speech in the Private and Public Workplace: Two Doctrines or One?" *Industrial Relations Journal,* 1 (Winter, 1977), 711.

McAdams, Tony. "Dismissal: A Decline in Employer Autonomy?" *Business Horizons,* February 1978, p. 67.

Maitland, Leslie. "Koch's Plan Strengthens Disciplining of Workers." *New York Times,* 6 March 1979, p. B1.

Palmer, David C. "Free Speech and Arbitration: Implications for the Future." *Labor Law Journal,* May 1976, p. 287.

Peck, Cornelius J. "Unjust Discharges from Employment: A Necessary Change in the Law." *Ohio State Law Journal,* 40 (1979), 1.

Rohweder, Ralph. "Education of a Whistle Blower." *The Washington Star,* 24 April 1978, p. A11.

Shapiro, J. Peter, and Tune, James F. "Implied Contract Rights to Job Security." *Stanford Law Review,* 26 (January 1974), 335.

Stessin, Lawrence. "Blue Collar Crime: Chewing Out the Boss." *New York Times,* 1 July 1979, p. F3.

Stevens, Charles W. "The Whistle Blower Chooses Hard Path." *Wall Street Journal,* 8 November 1978, p. 1.

Stieber, Jack. "Protection Against Unfair Dismissal." *Industrial Relations Newsletter,* Fall 1978, p. 4.

Stieber, Jack. "Speak Up, Get Fired." *New York Times,* 10 June 1979, p. E-19.

Summers, Clyde W. "Individual Protection Against Unjust Dismissal: Time For A Statute. *Virginia Law Review,* 62 (1976), 481.

Summers, Clyde W. "Protecting *All* Employees Against Unjust Dismissal," *Harvard Business Review,* Jan.-Feb. 1980, p. 132.

Vandivier, Kermit. "The Aircraft Brake Scandal." *Harper's Magazine,* April 1972, p. 45.

von Hippel, Frank. "Protecting the Whistle Blowers." *Physics Today,* October 1977, p. 9.

Walter, Kenneth. "Your Employee's Right to Blow the Whistle." *Harvard Business Review,* July-August 1975, p. 26.

## CASES

The following cases deal with charges of unjust dismissal and wrongful discharge brought by employees against private employers. The statutes are laws containing provisions forbidding employers to take reprisals against employees for reporting violations of the statute to the employer or public authorities.

*Agis v. Howard Johnson Company,* 355 N.E. 2d 315 (1976).

*Bernasconi v. Tempe Elementary School District,* 548 F. 2d 857 (9th Cir. 1977), cert. den. 434 U.S. 825.

*Bradington v. International Business Machine Corp.,* 360 F. Supp. 845 (1973).

*Brown v. Tanscon Lines,* 588 P. 2d 1087, (1978).

*Davis v. U.S. Steel Supply,* 581 F. 2d 335 (3rd Cir. 1978).

*Dockery v. Lampart Table Company,* 244 S.E. 2d 272 (1978).

*Donahue v. Staunton,* 471 F. 2d 475 (7th Cir. 1972).

*Donovan v. Reinbold,* 433 F. 2d 738 (9th Cir. 1970).

*Ebling v. Masco Corp.,* 261 N.W. 2d 74 (1977).

Edwards v. Citibank, 418 N.Y.S. 2d 269 (1979).

Geary v. U.S. Steel Corp., 319 A. 2d 174 (1974).

Gellert v. Eastern Air Lines, Inc., 370 S. 2d 802 (1979).

Givhan v. Western Line Consolidated School District, 439 U.S. 410 (1979).

Glenn v. Clearman's Golden Cock Inn, 192 C.A. 2d 793 (1961).

Harless v. First National Bank In Fairmont, 246 S.E. 2d 270 (1978).

Haurilak v. Kelley, 425 F. Supp. 626 (D. Conn. 1977).

Hinrichs v. Tranquilaire Hospital, 352 S.E. 2d 1138 (1977).

Holodnak v. Arco-Lycoming Division, 514 F. 2d 285 (2d Cir. 1975).

Jackson v. Minidaka Irrigation District, 563 P. 2d 54 (1977).

Johnson v. National Beef Packing Company, 551 P. 2d 779 (1976).

Kannisto v. City and Co. of San Francisco, 541 F. 2d 841 (9th Cir. 1976).

Kelsay v. Motorola, Inc., 366 N.E. 2d 1141, (1977).

Kenworth Trucks of Philadelphia v. NLRB, 580 F. 2d 55 (1978).

KLM Royal Dutch Airlines v. DeWit, 418 N.Y.S. 2d 63 (1979).

Larsen v. Motor Supply Co., 573 P. 2d 907 (1977).

Leach v. Lauhoff Grain Company, 366 N.E. 2d 1145 (1977).

Lewis v. Southeastern Pennsylvania Transportation Authority, 440 F. Supp. 887 (E.D. Pa. 1977).

Magri v. Giarrusso, 379 F. Supp. 353 (E.D. La. 1974).

Marshall v. Daniel Construction Company, 563 F. 2d 707, (5th Cir. 1977).

Marshall v. Whirlpool Corp., 593 F. 2d 715, (6th Cir. 1979).

Martin v. Platt, 386 N.E. 2d 1026 (1979).

McLellan v. Mississippi Power and Light Company, 545 F. 2d 919 (5th Cir. 1977).

Monge v. Beebe Rubber Company, 316 A. 2d 549 (1974).

Montalvo v. Zamora, 86 Cal. Rptr. 401 (1970).

Nees v. Hocks, 536 P. 2d 512 (1975).

O'Neil v. Ara Service Inc., 457 F. Supp. 182 (E.D. Pa. 1978).

O'Sullivan v. Mallon, 390 A. 2d 149 (1978).

Percival v. General Motors Corp., 539 F. 2d 1126 (8th Cir. 1976).

Perdue v. J. C. Penney, 470 F. Supp. 1234 (1979).

Petermann v. International Brotherhood, Etc., 344 P. 2d 25 (1959).

Pettway v. American Cast Iron Pipe Co., 411 F. 2d 998 (5th Cir. 1969).

Pickering v. Board of Education, 391 U.S. 563 (1968).

Pierce v. Ortho Pharmaceuticals, 166 N.J. Super. 335, 399 A. 2d 1023 (1979).

Pilarowski v. Brown, 257 N.W. 2d 211 (1977).

Pilkington v. Bevilacqua, 434 F. Supp. (D.R.I. 1977).

Pirre v. Printing Developments, Inc., 432 F. Supp. 840 (S.D. N.Y. 1977).

Porter v. Mathews, 428 F. Supp. 711 (N.D. Ala. 1976).

Rafferty v. Philadelphia Psychiatric Center, 356 F. Supp. 500, (E.D. Pa. 1973).

Reuther v. Fowler & Williams, Inc., 386 A. 2d 119 (1978).

Rost v. Horky, 422 F. Supp. 615 (D. Neb. 1976).

Rutherford v. American Bank of Commerce, 565 F. 2d 1162 (1977).

Scroghan v. Kraftko Corp., 551 S.W. 2d 811 (1977).

Shaw v. S. S. Kresge Company, 328 N.E. 2d 775 (1975).

Simpson v. Weeks, 570 F. 2d 240 (8th Cir. 1978).

Slotkin v. Human Development Corp. of Metropolitan St. Louis, 454 F. Supp. 250 (E.D. Mo. 1978).

Smith v. Singer, 19 F.E.P. Cases 1509 (N.D. Cal. 1979).

Sventko v. The Kroger Company, 69 Nich. App. 644 (1976).

*Tompkins v. Public Service Electric and Gas Co.,* 568 F. 2d 1044 (3d Cir. 1977).

*Trombetta v. Detroit, Toledo and Ironton R. Co.,* 265 N.W. 2d 385 (1978).

*Tygrett v. Washington,* 543 F. 2d 840 (D.C. Cir. 1974).

*West v. First National Bank of Atlanta,* 245 S.E. 2d 46 (1978).

*Women Employed v. Rinella & Rinella,* 19 F.E.P. Cases 712, (N.D. Ill. 1979).

## STATUTES

Age Discrimination Act of 1967, Pub. L.90–202, Sec. 4.

Civil Rights Act of 1964, Title VII, Pub. L. 88–352, Sec. 704.

Clean Air Act Amendments of 1977, Pub. L. 95–95, Sec. 312.

Connecticut Labor Code: Workmen's Compensation, Title 31, Sec. 379, "Discrimination Against Employee Filing Complaint."

Consumer Credit Protection Act of 1968, Pub. L. 90–321, Sec. 304.

Employee Retirement Income Security Act of 1974, Pub. L. 93–406, Sec. 510.

Farm Labor Contractor Registration Act Amendments of 1974, Pub. L. 93–518, Sec. 13(a).

Federal Mine Safety and Health Act of 1977, Pub. L. 164, Sec. 105(c).

Federal Water Pollution Control Act Amendments of 1972, Pub. L. 92–500, Sec. 507.

Illinois Employment Code: Workmen's Compensation, Chap. 48, Sec. 138.4(h), "Provision to Insure Payment Of Compensation."

Missouri Workmen's Compensation, Sec. 287.780, "Discrimination Against Employee For Exercise Of Rights."

New Jersey Labor and Workmen's Compensation Code, Title 34:15, Sec. 39.1, "Unlawful Discharge Of, Or Discrimination Against, Employee Claiming Compensation Benefits; Penalty."

Nuclear Regulatory Commission Authorization of 1978, Pub. L. 95–601, Sec. 10.

Occupational Safety and Health Act of 1970, Pub. L. No. 91–596, Sec. 11(c).

Oregon Labor and Industrial Relations Code: Workmen's Compensation, Chap. 659, Sec. 410, "Discrimination Against Workmen Applying For Workmen's Compensation Benefits Prohibited."

Resource Conservation and Recovery Act of 1976, Pub. L. 94–580, Sec. 7001.

Safe Drinking Water Act of 1974, Pub. L. 93–523, Sec. 1450.

Texas Workmen's Compensation Law, Vol. 22, Art. 8307C, "Protection of Claimants from Discrimination by Employers; Remedies, Jurisdiction."

Toxic Substances Control Act of 1976, Pub. L. 94–469, Sec. 23.

# Index